THE CATHOLIC UNIVERSITY OF AMERICA
CANON LAW STUDIES
No. 247

The Recipient of First Holy Communion

A HISTORICAL SYNOPSIS AND COMMENTARY

by

REV. MATTHEW M. CROTTY, J.C.L.
Priest of the Diocese of Baker City

A DISSERTATION

Submitted to the Faculty of the School of Canon Law of the Catholic University of America in Partial Fulfillment of the Requirements for the Degree of Doctor of Canon Law

THE CATHOLIC UNIVERSITY OF AMERICA PRESS
WASHINGTON, D. C.
1947

Nihil Obstat:

CLEMENS V. BASTNAGEL, S.T.L., J.U.D.,
Censor Deputatus.

Washingtonii, D. C., die 9 maii, 1947.

Imprimatur:

✠ IOSEPH F. MCGRATH, D.D.,
Episcopus Bakeriensis.

Bakeriae, die 17 maii, 1947.

Printed by
THE PAULIST PRESS
401 WEST 59TH STREET
NEW YORK 19, N. Y.

61

DEDICATED

TO

MY PARENTS

TABLE OF CONTENTS

PART II

CANONICAL COMMENTARY

CHAPTER III

CHAPTER IV

CHAPTER V

CHAPTER VI

CHAPTER VII

CHAPTER VIII

FOREWORD

LITTLE need be said by way of introduction to the subject matter of this dissertation. All Catholic priests and even the average Catholic layman are familiar in some degree with most of the problems which come up for discussion.

A word about the plan which is followed in the work may here be called for. The decree *Quam singulari,* issued by the Sacred Congregation of the Sacraments on August 8, 1910, may be described as the core about which the dissertation is built. This decree contains a concise and masterly survey of the legislation and custom which governed the reception of first Holy Communion from the earliest times until the twentieth century.

In his historical synopsis the writer expands and illustrates the statements contained in the decree, and in addition discusses some aspects of the subject not touched on by the Sacred Congregation. The decree is likewise of paramount importance as regards the canonical commentary, inasmuch as the norms which it contains form the immediate basis for those canons of the Code which now regulate the reception of first Holy Communion. The norms furnished by the decree *Quam singulari* are an indispensable means for the proper interpretation of the corresponding canons.

The writer takes this occasion to extend a most sincere expression of gratitude to His Excellency, Joseph F. McGrath, Bishop of Baker City, for the opportunity of advanced study in Canon Law, and for his many acts of kindness in connection with the work; to the members of the Faculty of the School of Canon Law for their direction and assistance; and to all others who have in any way contributed toward the completion of this dissertation.

Part One

Historical Synopsis

CHAPTER I

FROM THE II CENTURY TO THE COUNCIL OF TRENT (1545-1563)

Article 1. Legislation Prior to the IV General Council of the Lateran (1215)

From the earliest times until the thirteenth century it was customary to allow children who had not yet reached the use of reason to receive Holy Communion. In the writings of ecclesiastics and in the ancient Sacramentaries and *Ordines* there is abundant evidence to prove that for twelve centuries the reception of the Eucharist by young neophytes formed part of the ceremony of baptism. Hence to a great extent the early history of the reception of Holy Communion by children is the history of the ceremonies connected with the conferring of the sacrament of baptism.

This practice was prevalent throughout both the East and the West. Children were considered as having a right to the reception of the Body and Blood of Christ by the fact of being made members of Christ at baptism.[1] In the Western Church the custom disappeared at the time of the IV General Council of the Lateran (1215). It still survives in the East among Greeks and Orientals, at least in certain localities. On June 16, 1761, the Holy Office in reply to a request that the custom should be suppressed where it was still in vogue stated that no change should be made.[2]

[1] Corblet, *Histoire Dogmatique, Liturgique et Archéologique du Sacrement de L'Eucharistie* (2 vols., Paris: Societé Générale de Librairie Catholique, 1885), I, 304.

[2] *Collectanae S. Congregationis de Propaganda Fide* (2 vols., Romae: Typographis Polyglotta S.C. de Propaganda Fide, 1907), n. 713 (hereafter cited *Collect.*).

St. Justin Martyr (c. 100—c. 165) was one of the earliest ecclesiastical writers to refer to the custom of communicating neophytes immediately after baptism. He stated that when the sacrament of baptism had been conferred the Body and Blood of Christ was consecrated and all present communicated.[3]

Tertullian (160?-230?) spoke of neophytes receiving the Eucharist and a drink composed of milk and honey.[4] This drink of milk and honey was used exclusively in the Romano-Alexandrian Rite, and was given to neophytes after they had received Holy Communion.[5] In explaining the significance of the potion to Senarius, a senator at the time of Theodoric (454-526), John the Deacon incidentally bore testimony to the fact that neophytes received Holy Communion.[6]

To obviate the danger of irreverence, Holy Communion was given exclusively under the species of wine to infants who were still being breast-fed.[7] The minister who conferred baptism dipped his finger in the consecrated wine and allowed the infant to suck the

[3] *Apologia II*—Martène, *De Antiquis Ecclesiae Ritibus* (4 vols., Rotomagi: Sumptibus Guillelmi Behourt, 1700), I, 143.

[4] *Adversus Marcionem I*, c. 14—"Sed ille quidem usque nunc nec aquam reprobavit Creatoris, qua suos abluit; nec oleum, quo suos unguit; nec mellis et lactis societatem, qua suos infantat; nec panem, quo ipsum corpus suum repraesentat."—Migne, *Patrologiae Cursus Completus, Series Latina* (221 vols., Parisiis, 1844-1864), II, 262 (hereafter cited *MPL*); *Liber de Corona*, c. 3—"Inde suscepti, lactis et mellis concordiam praegustamus: exque ea die, lavacro quotidiano per totam hebdomadem abstinemus. Eucharistiae sacramentum, et in tempore victus, et omnibus mandatum a Domino. . . ."—*MPL*, II, 79.

[5] Duchesne, *Christian Worship, its origin and evolution*: translated from the third French edition by M. L. McClure (London: Society for Promoting Christian Knowledge, 1903), p. 333.

[6] "Baptizatis ergo hoc sacramenti genus offertur, ut intelligant quia non alii, sed ipsi participes fiunt corporis et sanguinis Domini terram repromissionis accipiunt."—*MPL*, LIX, 405.

[7] S. C. de Sacr., decr. 8 aug. 1910—*Acta Apostolicae Sedis, Commentarium Officiale* (Romae, 1909-1929; Civitate Vaticana, 1929—), II (1910), 78 (hereafter cited *AAS*); *Codicis Iuris Canonici Fontes*, cura Emi Petri Card. Gasparri editi (9 vols., Romae—Civitate Vaticana: Typis Polyglottis Vaticanis, 1923-1939. Vols. VII-IX, ed. cura et studio Emi Iustiniani Card. Serédi), n. 2103 (hereafter cited *Fontes*).

drops adhering thereto.[8] Corblet (1819-1886) disagreed with writers who maintained that children received Holy Communion under the species of wine alone. He asserted that there was no positive text to prove their contention, and that children were often not baptized until they were one year old, when they could eat bread.[9] His view was not necessarily opposed to the teaching contained in the decree *Quam singulari,* if it is taken to mean that children who could eat bread did not receive under the species of wine alone. The decree uses the word *lactentes* to denote the type of infant who received under the species of wine alone.

Numerous references to the fact that neophytes received the Eucharist immediately after baptism may be found in the writings of St. Cyprian of Carthage (+258). According to him the Eucharist was administered to the newly baptized under the species of wine.[10] In his *Liber de Lapsis* he spoke of a deacon giving the consecrated wine to an infant.[11] Parents who allowed their children to die without receiving the Eucharist would, according to St. Cyprian, be held responsible on the day of judgment.[12]

Among the Greek Fathers, St. Cyril of Jerusalem (315?-386) testified that the anointing with chrism and the reception of the Eucharist were part of the baptismal ceremony.[13]

It can likewise be deduced from the writing of St. John Chrysostom (347?-407) that Holy Communion was given to neophytes.

[8] Cappello, *De aetate admittendorum ad primam Communionem Eucharisticam* (Romae: Typis Cuggiani, 1911), p. 19.

[9] *Histoire Dogmatique et Archéologique du Sacrement de L'Eucharistie,* I, 305.

[10] *Epistola LXIII* (Ad Caecilium): "Per Baptismum enim Spiritus sanctus accipitur et sic a baptizatis et Spiritum sanctum consecutis ad bibendum calicem Domini pervenitur."—*MPL,* IV, 380.

[11] *MPL,* IV, 485.

[12] *Liber de Lapsis*—"Nonne illi cum iudicii dies venerit dicent: Nos nihil male fecimus, nec, derelicto cibo et poculo Domini ad profana contagia sponte properavimus. Perdidit nos aliena perfidia, parentes sensimus parricidas."—*MPL,* IV, 473.

[13] *Catechesis Mystagogica XXIII*—Migne, *Patrologiae Cursus Completus, Series Graeca* (161 vols., Parisiis: 1856-1866), XXXIII, 1110.

Just as a mother hastens to nourish her offspring, he wrote, so Christ nourishes with His Blood those whom He has regenerated.[14] The "regeneration" referred to rebirth in the waters of baptism.

According to a writer who for centuries was identified with Dionysius the Areopagite, but who lived during the latter half of the fifth century, the reception of Holy Communion in the baptismal ceremony followed the anointing with chrism.[15]

In nearly all the ancient liturgical books written before the twelfth century mention is made of the custom of communicating little children at the time of their baptism.[16] Two types of liturgical books are useful for the purpose of the present work; the *Ordines,* which contained merely ritual directions for different ceremonies,[17] and the Sacramentaries, which contained both directions and prayers for liturgical functions. The collections of the *Ordines Romani* by J. Mabillon (1632-1707) and of various local *Ordines* by E. Martène (1654-1739) are most important for the matter of tracing the ceremonies connected with the conferring of baptism.[18]

The ancient *Ordo* of the Church of Apamea in Syria, written about the year 500, directed that children should receive the Eucharist fasting immediately after being baptized. Only in cases of necessity could they be suckled before receiving, and they were expected to be present at Mass and to receive Holy Communion every day during the following week.[19]

[14] *Homilia ad Neophytos*—"Sicut mulier affectionis natura agente genitum alere sui lactis foecunditate festinat, sic et Christus, quos ipse regenerat, suo Sanguine enutrit."—Maringola, *Antiquitatum Christianarum Institutiones* (2. ed., 2 vols., Neapoli: Pelella, 1862), II, 360.

[15] *Liber Secundus de Ecclesiastica Hierarchia—MPL,* CXXII, 1076.

[16] S. C. de Sacramentis, decr. 8 aug. 1910—*AAS,* II (1910), 578; *Fontes,* n. 2103.

[17] Duchesne, *Christian Worship, its origin and evolution,* p. 146.

[18] Oppenheim, *Institutiones systematico-historicae in Sacram Liturgiam,* Pars II, *Liturgia specialis,* Series II, *Liturgia Sacramentalis* (*Ritualis et Pontificalis*), Vol. I, *De fontibus et historia ritus baptismalis* (Taurini-Romae: Marietti, 1943), I, 26 (hereafter cited *De fontibus et historia ritus baptismalis*).

[19] *Ordo XIV*: "Illud de parvulis providendum est, ne postquam baptizati fuerint, ullum cibum accipiant, nec ablectantur sine summa necessitate antequam communicent sacramento Corporis Christi. Et postea totam hebdomadam

Similar regulations were in force in Rome, but with this difference that no exception was made to the law of fast even for cases of necessity. The Roman regulations read as follows:

> Illud autem de parvulis providendum est, ut, postquam baptizati fuerint, nullum cibum accipiant, nec lactentur, antequam communicent sacramenta corporis Christi: et omnibus diebus septimae Paschae ad Missas procedant, et parentes eorum offerant pro ipsis, et communicent omnes. Hunc autem supradictum ordinem baptismi, in hoc sabbato Paschae sicut in sabbato Pentecostes omnimodo celebratur.[20]

Critics have assigned no definite date to the composition of this *Ordo*. Duchesne (1843-1922) remarked that it must be very ancient, inasmuch as it did not correspond to the ceremonies in use in Rome in 832.[21]

In France, before the advent of Charlemagne (742-814) to the throne, the most widely used liturgical book was a work known as the Gelasian Sacramentary. No weight can be attached to the name "Gelasian." The sacramentary must be understood as a Roman Liturgical collection introduced into France some time before the pontificate of Pope Adrian I (772-795), but after the death of Pope Gregory the Great (590-604). As it is now known the book has undergone many modifications in a Gallican direction.[22] The Roman original was written most probably in the seventh or in the early years of the eighth century.[23]

With regard to the reception of Holy Communion by infant neophytes the Gelasian Sacramentary prescribed:

> Postea, quum ascenderit a fonte, infans signatur a presbytero in cerebro de chrismate, his verbis. . . . Postea, si fuerit oblata,

paschae omnibus diebus ad missam procedant, offerant et communicent. Hic autem suprascriptus ordo baptismi, sicut in sabbato paschae, sic et in sabbato Pentecostes celebretur."—Martène, *De Antiquis Ecclesiae Ritibus*, I, 198.

[20] *Ordo Primus Romanus*, n. 46—Mabillon, *Musaeum Italicum* (2 vols., Parisiis: Montelant, 1724), II, 3.

[21] *Christian Worship, its origin and evolution*, p. 147.

[22] Duchesne, *op. cit.*, pp. 129-134.

[23] Wilson, *The Gelasian Sacramentary* (Oxford: Clarendon Press, 1894), p. xvii.

> agendae sunt missae, et communicat; sin autem, dabis ei tantum sacramenta corporis et sanguinis Christi, dicens: Corpus Domini nostri Christi sit tibi in vitam aeternam.[24]

When Charlemagne (742-814) ascended the Frankish Throne he instituted a reformation in Church discipline. One of the aspects of this reformation was the co-ordination of liturgical observances. Charlemagne requested Pope Adrian I (772-795) to send him a Roman sacramentary. Between the years 784 and 791 a work known as the Gregorian Sacramentary was dispatched to France. Charlemagne had many copies of this sacramentary made, and all the churches in the Frankish dominions were obliged to use it. But this Gregorian Sacramentary did not contain all the details and formularies needed for the carrying out of church functions, and hence it was combined with the Gelasian Sacramentary. It would seem that the name "Gregorian" is a misnomer, since the time of composition of the original work must be placed prior to the time of Gregory the Great (c. 540-604).[25]

In it provision was made for the reception of Holy Communion by the newly baptized infant. The following rubric is relevant to the practice:

> Et vestitur Infans vestimentis suis. Si vero Episcopus adest, statim confirmare eum oportet Chrismate, et postea Communicare. Et si Episcopus deest, Communicetur a Presbytero, dicente ita: Corpus Domini nostri Jesu Cristi custodiat te in vitam aeternam. Amen.[26]

This portion of the Gregorian Sacramentary is purely Roman and contained no Frankish interpolations.[27] Hence from this Sacramentary it can be deduced that at the time of Charlemagne, both in Rome and in France, it was customary to communicate infant neophytes immediately after baptism.

[24] Lib. I, c. 75—*Ibid.*, p. 117.

[25] Duchesne, *Christian Worship, its origin and evolution*, pp. 120-123.

[26] Muratori, *Liturgia Romana Vetus* (2 vols., Neapoli: Typis Cajetani Castellani, 1776), II, 73.

[27] Duchesne, *op. cit.*, p. 122, footnote.

Further proof of the existence of this custom in Rome may be obtained from *Ordo Romanus VII.* Duchesne remarked that, though this *Ordo* was published from ninth century manuscripts, it must have been written at the latest in the early years of the eighth century.[28] The provisions of this *Ordo* with regard to the communicating of infants were substantially the same as those contained in the *Ordo Romanus I.*[29]

Sometime during the latter years of his life Charlemagne required the bishops and other learned men of his kingdom to write to him describing the ceremonies in use in various localities in connection with the administration of the sacrament of baptism.[30] Among the responses which show that the reception of Holy Communion by neophytes was part of the baptismal ceremony as observed at that time were those of Maxentius, Bishop of Aquileia (+836),[31] of Leidardus, Bishop of Lyons (+813),[32] and of Amalarius, Archbishop of Treves (+ca. 816).[33]

A French *Ordo,* written about the year 900, repeated the instructions of the Roman *Ordines,* which required infant neophytes to receive the Eucharist immediately after baptism while still fasting, and which demanded also that they attend Mass daily and receive Holy Communion during the octave of Easter.[34]

[28] *Op. cit.,* p. 149.

[29] N. 12: "Post hoc ingrediuntur ad Missas, et communicant omnes ipsos infantes; illud providentes, ut postquam baptizati fuerint, nullum cibum accipiant, nec ablectentur, antequam communicant. . . . Hoc autem supra scripto ordine baptismi, sicut in Sabbato sancto Paschae, sic et sabbato Pentecosten omnimodis celebretur."—Mabillon, *Musaeum Italicum,* II, 83.

[30] Oppenheim, *De fontibus et historia ritus baptismalis,* p. 12.

[31] *Epistola ad Carolum Magnum Imperatorem de significatu Rituum Baptismi—MPL,* CVI, 53-54.

[32] *Liber de Sacramento Baptismi ad Carolum Magnum Imperatorem*—"Oportet renovatos per baptismum mensae Dominicae applicari, ut sumentes panem qui cor hominis confirmat, et vinum quod laetificat, dicere possint cum Psalmista: . . ."—*MPL,* IC, 866.

[33] *Epistola ad Carolum Magnum Imperatorem de Caeremoniis Baptismi—MPL,* IC, 899.

[34] *Ordo VIII,* ex codice S. Remigii Remensis—"Post hoc ingrediuntur ad Missas, illud praevidentes, ut postquam baptizati fuerint, nullum cibum accipi-

The reception of Holy Communion by little children was not confined to the reception on the day of their baptism and during the following seven days. They continued to receive the Eucharist after baptism and before attaining the use of reason. In some churches the custom was to communicate them immediately after the clerics had received, while in other places they communicated after the adults.[85]

St. Augustine (354-430) spoke of infants receiving Holy Communion without making any reference to the conferring of the sacrament of baptism. He wrote:

> Infantes sunt, sed membra eius fiunt. Infantes sunt, sed Sacramenta eius accipiunt. Infantes sunt, sed mensae eius participes fiunt, ut habeant in se vitam.[86]

He mentioned the fact that sometimes children received the Eucharist under the species of wine only, and sometimes under the species of bread.[87] Since only the *lactentes* received under the species of wine alone, it can be concluded that the children spoken of by St. Augustine as receiving under the species of bread were children of a somewhat more advanced age.

Evagrius the historian (ca. 536-ca. 600) told of an ancient custom which existed in Constantinople. If many consecrated particles remained over after the celebration of Mass, then boys and girls of a tender age were summoned to consume them.[88] A similar practice was approved by the National Council of Mâcon (585). The Council decreed:

ant, nec ablactantur antequam communicent. Et omnibus diebus septem paschae semper ad missas procedant. Et offeruntur pro ipsis, et communicant omnes."—Martène, *De Antiquis Ecclesiae Ritibus,* I, 180.

[85] S. C. de Sacramentis, decr. 8 aug. 1910—*AAS,* II (1910), 578; *Fontes,* n. 2103.

[86] *Sermo CLXXIV—MPL,* XXXVIII, 944.

[87] *Opus Imperfectum contra Julianum,* Lib. II, c. 30—*MPL,* XLV, 1154; *Epistola CCXVII—MPL,* XXXIII, 984.

[88] *A History of the Church in six books from A. D. 431 to A. D. 594.* A New Translation from the Greek (London: Samuel Bagster & Sons, 1846), Book IV, chap. 6, p. 235.

> Quaecumque reliquiae sacrificiorum post peractam Missam in sacrario supersederint, quarta vel sexta feria innocentes ab illo cuius interest ad ecclesiam abducantur, et indicto eis ieunio easdem reliquias conspersas vino percipiant.[39]

Cappello was of the opinion that the *innocentes* referred to by the Council were little children incapable of evil.[40] In other words, the children invited to consume the Sacred Species were those who had not yet attained the use of reason.

From a decree of the XI Provincial Council of Toledo (675) it can be deduced that in Spain also it was customary to communicate children between the time of their baptism and the time of their attainment of the use of reason. The Council ruled that children could not be punished if during the period of their infancy they vomited the Eucharist.[41]

It seems that the Carolingian period was the turning point for the Latin Church in the history of the custom of communicating children immediately after baptism. Evidence of the widespread existence of the custom is most abundant during this period, as has already been shown. In the eleventh century there were numerous exceptions to the practice, and the number of these exceptions continued to grow until the custom disappeared during the thirteenth century in the West.[42]

Some evidence of the continued existence of the ancient custom into the middle of the twelfth century is found. William of Champeaux (c. 1070-1121) referred to the fact that newly baptized children received only the Precious Blood when communicating, since

[39] C. 6—Mansi, *Sacrorum Conciliorum Nova et Amplissima Collectio* (53 vols. in 60, Paris-Leipzig-Arnhem, 1901-1927), IX, 853 (hereafter cited Mansi).

[40] *De Aetate admittendorum ad primam Communionem Eucharisticam*, p. 19.

[41] C. 11—"Quicumque ergo fidelis inevitabili qualibet infirmitate coactus, eucharistiam perceptam reiecerit, in nullo ecclesiasticae damnationis subiaceat. Similiter nec illos cuiusquam punitionis censura redarguet, qui talia tempore infantiae faciunt. . . ."—Mansi, XI, 144.

[42] Corblet, *Histoire Dogmatique, Liturgique et Archéologique du Sacrement de L'Eucharistie*, I, 307.

they could not eat bread.[43] According to Hugh of St. Victor (1096-1141) it was still customary for the minister to dip his finger in the consecrated Wine and to allow the infant to suck the drops adhering to it.[44] Gilbert of Poitiers (c. 1076-1154) likewise mentioned the fact that recently baptized children often received the Eucharist solely under the species of Wine.[45]

Article 2. The Decree *Omnis utriusque*

With the cessation of the old practice of communicating infant neophytes a new discipline arose in the Church. Children were not admitted to receive the Eucharist until they enjoyed in some measure the use of reason and had some knowledge of the Sacrament.[46] This new discipline received the solemn sanction of the Church in the IV General Council of the Lateran (1215). The right and the obligation to receive the Eucharist thenceforth began when children had reached the years of discretion. The decree of the Council read as follows:

> Omnis utriusque sexus fidelis, postquam ad annos discretionis pervenerit, omnia sua peccata confiteatur fideliter, saltem semel in anno proprio sacerdoti, et iniunctam sibi poenitentiam studeat pro viribus adimplere, suscipiens reverenter ad minus in Pascha Eucharistiae sacramentum, nisi forte de consilio proprii sacerdotis ob aliquam rationabilem causam ad tempus ab eius perceptione duxerit abstinendum.[47]

The Council did not prohibit the ancient custom of communicating infants at the time of baptism; nevertheless, it marked the beginning of the new practice in the Latin Church of deferring the reception of the Eucharist until the years of discretion were reached.

[43] *De Sacramento Altaris*—"Unde et infantulis mox baptizatis solus calix datur, quia pane uti non possunt. . . . "—*MPL*, CLXIII, 1039.

[44] *De Sacramentis*, lib. I, c. 20—"Pueris recens natis idem sacramentum in specie sanguinis est ministrandum, digito sacerdotis, quia tales naturaliter sugere possunt."—Maringola, *Antiquitatum Christianarum Institutiones*, II, 361.

[45] *Epistola ad Matthaeum Abbatem S. Florentii—MPL*, CLXXXVIII, 1256.

[46] S. C. de Sacramentis, decr. 8 aug. 1910—*AAS*, II (1910), 578; *Fontes*, n. 2103.

[47] Mansi, XXX, 1007; Schroeder, *Disciplinary Decrees of the General Councils* (St. Louis: Herder, 1937), p. 570.

Centuries later, theologians disagreed widely on the precise meaning of the phrase "*annos discretionis.*" The correct interpretation of the phrase was the interpretation given to it by councils and theologians contemporaneous to the IV Lateran Council.

The decree *Omnis utriusque* is found repeated in the Decretals of Gregory IX (1227-1241). The gloss to the word *discretionis* explained that a child reached the age of discretion when it became *capax doli,* that is, when it became capable of committing sin.[48] According to the Council of Rouen (1235) no priest was to give Holy Communion to any child under seven years of age.[49] St. Thomas Aquinas (1226-1274) was lauded in the decree *Quam singulari*[50] as accurately interpreting the meaning of the Fathers of the IV Lateran Council when he taught that children could be admitted to the reception of the Eucharist when they began to have enough use of reason to enable them to conceive a devotion towards the Sacrament of the Altar.[51] The Eucharist, he taught, should not be given to children who were unable to distinguish spiritual from material bread. It was allowable to communicate children in whom signs of discretion and devotion were apparent, even though they had not yet reached the full age of discretion.[52] A decree very similar in tenor to that of the Council of Rouen was enacted in the year

[48] C. 12, X, *de poenitentiis et remissionibus,* V, 38—"id est, cum est doli capax: quia tunc potest peccare. . . ."—*Decretales D. Gregorii Papae IX, una cum Glossis restitutae* (Romae, 1582).

[49] C. 21—"Prohibetur Presbyteris ne hostias dent pueris ullo modo infra septennium constitutis."—Mansi, XXIII, 376.

[50] *AAS,* II (1910), 580; *Fontes,* n. 2103.

[51] "Quando pueri incipiunt aliqualem usum rationis habere ut possint devotionem concipere huius sacramenti, tunc potest eis hoc sacramentum conferri."—*Summa Theologica,* Pars III, q. 80, a. 9, ad 3 (12. ed., 6 vols., Taurini: Marietti, 1937-1938), V, 183.

[52] *In IV Libros Sententiarum,* dist. IX, q. 1, art. 5, solutio 4: "Dicendum quod pueris carentibus usu rationis, qui non possunt distinguere inter cibum spiritualem et corporalem non debet Eucharistia dari. . . . Pueris autem iam incipientibus habere discretionem etiam ante perfectam aetatem, puta cum sint decem vel undecim annorum aut circa hoc, potest dari, si in eis signa discretionis appareant et devotionis."—*Opera Omnia, studio et labore Stanislai Edwardi Frette et Pauli Mare* (34 vols., Vol. X, Parisiis: Vives, 1837), X, 230.

1300 by the Council of Bayeaux. This decree likewise prohibited priests from admitting children under seven years of age to the reception of Holy Communion.[53]

The new discipline introduced by the IV General Council of the Lateran had a widespread effect. Many local councils brought it to the immediate attention of pastors by embodying it in their legislation.[54]

[53] C. 16—"Inhibemus presbyteris ne hostias dent pueris ullo modo infra septennium constitutis."—Mansi, XXV, 63.

[54] Council of Toulouse (1229), cap. 13—Mansi, XXIII, 197; Council of Sens (1269), c. 4—Mansi, XXIV, 5; Hardouin, *Acta Conciliorum et Epistolae Decretales ac Constitutiones Summorum Pontificum* (12 vols., Parisiis, 1714-1715), VII, 650 (hereafter cited Hardouin); Council of Saint Omer (1279), c. 5—Mansi, XXIV, 222; Hardouin, VII, 767; Council of Münster (1279), cap. 17—Mansi, XXIV, 318; Council of Béziers (1286), cap. 13—Mansi, XXIV, 632; Council of Benevento (1331), cap. 66—Mansi, XXV, 971.

CHAPTER II

FROM THE COUNCIL OF TRENT (1545-1563) TO THE CODE OF CANON LAW (1918)

Article 1. The Age of Discretion

Section 1. Legislation Prior to 1910

The Council of Trent (1545-1563) reaffirmed substantially the legislation of the IV General Council of the Lateran (1215) regarding the reception of Holy Communion by children, and in addition passed much new legislation on the matter. It declared anathema anyone who denied that the faithful of both sexes were bound to the annual reception of the Eucharist at least during the Paschal season.[1] The Council likewise declared anathema anyone who held that not each and everyone of the faithful of both sexes was obliged by the precept of annual confession according to the constitution of the Lateran Council.[2]

The Fathers of the Council stressd the fact that children who still lacked the use of reason were not obliged to receive Holy Communion. They did not condemn the earlier Fathers who followed

[1] Sess. XIII, *de Eucharistia,* can. 9: "Si quis negaverit, omnes et singulos Christi fideles utriusque sexus, cum ad annos discretionis pervenerint, teneri singulis annis saltem in Paschate ad communicandum iuxta praeceptum sanctae matris ecclesiae: anathema sit."—Schroeder, *Canons and Decrees of the Council of Trent* (St. Louis: Herder, 1941), p. 356; Denzinger-Bannwart-Umberg, *Enchiridion Symbolorum, Definitionum et Declarationum de Rebus Fidei et Morum* (21.-23. ed., Friburgi Brisgoviae: Herder, 1937), nn. 933 and 937 (hereafter cited Denzinger).

[2] Sess. XIV, *de Poenitentia,* can. 8: "Si quis dixerit, confessionem omnium peccatorum, qualem ecclesia servat, esse impossibilem, et traditionem humanam a piis abolendam; aut ad eam non teneri omnes et singulos utriusque sexus Christi fideles iuxta magni concilii Lateranensis constitutionem semel in anno, et ob id suadendum esse Christi fidelibus, ut non confiteantur tempore Quadragesimae: anathema sit"; Schroeder, *Canons and Decrees of the Council of Trent,* p. 378.

the custom of giving the Eucharist to children before they had attained the use of reason, but declared that it was certain and beyond controversy that the Fathers who did this in no way believed that it was necessary for salvation.[3] Finally, the Council declared anathema anyone who taught that the Eucharist was necessary for children who had not yet reached the age of discretion.[4]

A special problem confronted the theologians. How was it to be determined that children had arrived at the years of discretion which implied for them the obligation of at least annually receiving Holy Communion? Opinion was divided on the question. Some held that a distinction should be made between the age of discretion relative to the precept of the annual reception of Holy Communion, and the age of discretion relative to the precept of the annual reception of the sacrament of penance. Others held that the age was the same for both precepts.

Adherents of the first school of thought based their opinion to some extent on the wording of the decree *Omnes utriusque* of the IV General Council of the Lateran (1215), which declared that all the faithful of both sexes, when they reached the age of discretion, had to faithfully confess their sins at least once a year, and to reverently receive Holy Communion at least at Easter.[5] They argued that the word *reverenter* implied a qualification which postulated a more advanced age for the reception of first Holy Communion than for the reception of sacramental absolution.

De Lugo (1583-1660) discussed the various opinions concerning the age of discretion. Some understood it as the age of puberty. Others taught that the obligation to receive did not begin to bind until the age of twelve. Others held that more was desired for the reception of the Eucharist than for the making of a sacramental confession: children should confess when they first know how to sin, but should not receive the Eucharist until they could distinguish

[3] Sess. XXI, *de Communione*, c. 4—Schroeder, *op. cit.*, p. 408.

[4] Sess. XXI, *de Communione*, can. 4: "Si quis dixerit, parvulis, antequam ad annos discretionis pervenerint, necessariam esse Eucharistiae communionem: anathema sit."—Schroeder, *op. cit.*, p. 409.

[5] Cf. *supra*, p. 10 for pertinent text.

It from common bread and adore the Divine Majesty latent in the sacrament: children were commonly regarded as being able to do this between their twelfth and fourteenth year.[6]

De Lugo himself taught that children were obliged to receive Holy Communion when they could distinguish the Eucharist from other food. This they could usually do when they became capable of sinning or shortly afterwards. Outside the danger of death children were not bound to receive Holy Communion immediately after becoming qualified to do so. Thus, for example, it would be quite licit for them, acting on their confessor's advice, to defer the reception of the Eucharist for a year, so that they could prepare themselves to receive It with greater reverence.[7]

Suarez (1548-1617) took exception to the opinion of Dominicus de Soto (1494-1560) who had taught that, since no ecclesiastical precepts bound children until they had reached the age of twelve, they were likewise not obliged to communicate until they had reached that age. Suarez pointed out that certain other ecclesiastical precepts bound children before they attained that age. He agreed with Soto's view that there was no obligation for children to receive for a year or two after they could licitly do so.[8]

St. Alphonsus Liguori (1696-1787) taught that children neither could nor should receive Holy Communion immediately after attaining the use of reason. At that age they were indeed bound to the precept of annual confession, but they were not on that account bound to the precept of receiving the blessed Eucharist, which is of

[6] *De Sacramento Eucharistiae,* disp. 13, sect. 4, n. 33—*Disputationes Scholasticae et Morales* (ed. nova, 8 vols., Parisiis: Vivès, 1868-1869), IV, 61-62.

[7] "Fateor itaque pueros non obligari divino praecepto, nisi sciant distinguere Eucharistiam ab aliis cibis: assero tamen id fere evenire quando habent usum rationis ad peccandum, vel paulo post; . . . Unde infero tempus obligationis non incipere pueris in indivisibili, sed potius esse multos quibus licite potest et hoc anno, v.g., dari Communio, eo quod iam habeant in toto rigore capacitatem sufficientem ad discernendum hoc sacramentum ab aliis cibis, et tamen licite potest illis differi Communio arbitrio confessarii ad annum sequentem ut melius et cum maiore reverentia se praeparent."—*De Sacramento Eucharistiae,* disp. 13, sect. 4, n. 39—*op. cit.,* IV, 63.

[8] *De Eucharistia,* q. 80, art. 11, disp. 70, sect. 1—*Opera Omnia* (ed. nova, 28 vols., Parisiis: Vivès, 1856-1866), XXI, 543.

greater excellence, but not so necessary. He followed the common opinion, which stated that children should not receive until they had completed their ninth or tenth year.[9]

The exponents of the view that children should receive immediately after attaining the use of reason followed the doctrine of St. Thomas (1225-1274), who taught that as soon as children began to have some use of reason which enabled them to conceive a devotion towards the Sacrament It could be given to them.[10] Vasquez (1551-1604) taught that the obligation to receive the blessed Eucharist began to bind children immediately after they had attained the use of reason, that is, when they could distinguish It from other food.[11]

According to the Spanish theologian, Fernando Castropalao (1581-1633) the use of reason regularly comes at the completion of the seventh year, when children begin to be bound by the ecclesiastical precepts. In his opinion there was no distinction between the age for confession and the age for Communion.[12]

Peter Ledesma (+1616), whose opinion was subsequently quoted *verbatim* in the decree *Quam singulari,* asserted that the Eucharist should be given to all who enjoyed the use of reason no matter how early it came, and even though the child still had but a confused knowledge of what it was doing.[13]

The austerity which accompanied the deferred administration of Holy Communion to children from the middle of the seventeenth century to the beginning of the twentieth has been attributed in some part to the baneful influence of Jansenism.[14] Jansenism de-

[9] *Theologia Moralis* (4 vols., Taurini: Marietti, 1872), Lib. VI, *de Eucharistia,* n. 301.

[10] Cf. *supra,* p. 11.

[11] *Libri Commentariorum in Tertiam Partem S. Thomae* (9 vols., Lugduni: Sumptibus Jacobi Cardon, 1630-1631), III, 350.

[12] *De Legibus,* tract. 3, disp. 1, punct. 24, n. 2—*Opera Omnia* (7 vols., Lugduni: Barbier, 1682), I, 114-115.

[13] "Dico ex omnium consensu quod omnibus habentibus usum rationis est danda Eucharistia quantumcumque cito habeant illum usum rationis, esto, quod adhuc confuse cognoscat ille puer quid faciat."—In *S. Th.,* q. 80, a. 9, ad 6; *Fontes,* n. 2103.

[14] S. C. de Sacramentis, decr. 8 aug. 1910—*AAS,* II (1910), 580; *Fontes,* n. 2103.

rives its name and origin from Cornelius Jansenius (1585-1638), Bishop of Ypres (1636-1638), whose work *Augustinus,* published in 1640 after his death, restated the errors of Luther (1483-1546) and Baius (1513-1589) concerning grace.[15]

Jansenius' intimate friend, Jean Du Vergier (1581-1643), wrote a treatise attacking frequent Communion, and this was answered by a Jesuit priest, Father de Sesmaisons.[16] In defense of Du Vergier's work Antoine Arnauld (1612-1694) published in 1643 a work entitled "On frequent Communion." [17] According to Arnauld, freedom from mortal and venial sin was not enough for communicating worthily: a degree of perfection was required superior to that of Christians of the Apostolic Age.[18]

The work was approved by many bishops and archbishops in France, who wrote to the Holy See saying that it was doing much good.[19] This may account for the fact that the work itself was never condemned.[20] However, various errors of Jansenius, on whose work Arnauld's book was based, were repeatedly condemned.[21]

To such excesses did the followers of Jansenius go that some of them refrained from fulfilling their Easter duty, and even refused Viaticum when dying.[22] In the diocese of Troyes the ceremony of first Holy Communion was entirely abolished.[23] It is not sur-

[15] Cf. Tanquerey, *Synopsis Theologiae Dogmaticae* (22. ed., 3 vols., Parisiis: Desclée, 1930), III, 33.

[16] Cf. Ferreres, *The Decree on Daily Communion,* English translation by H. Jiminez (St. Louis: Herder, 1909), p. 80.

[17] Ferreres, *loc. cit.*

[18] Cf. Petavius, *Dogmata Theologica* (8 vols., ed. nova, Parisiis: Vivès, 1866-1868), VIII, 295.

[19] Ferreres, *op. cit.,* p. 81.

[20] Cigno, *Giovanni Andrea Serrao e il Giansenismo nell' Italia Meridionale* (Palermo: Scuola Tipografica R. Istituto d'Assistenzo, 1938), p. 231.

[21] Innocentius X, const. *Cum occasione,* 31 maii 1653—Denzinger, nn. 1092-1096; Alexander VII, const. *Ad sacram beati Petri Sedem,* 16 oct. 1656—Denzinger, n. 1098; S. C. S. Off., decr. 7 dec. 1690—Denzinger, nn. 1291-1321; *Fontes,* n. 760.

[22] Cigno, *op. cit.,* p. 237.

[23] Rapin, *Memoirs* (2 vols., Paris: Gaume Freres et J. Duprey, 1865), II, 521.

prising, then, that Jansenism, though it was condemned, nevertheless influenced in some degree the conception of the age at which children were to communicate.

Many of the synods and councils held throughout Europe and America during the nineteenth century legislated on the age at which children should receive their first Holy Communion. Practically all of them insisted that children be allowed to communicate when they were old enough to distinguish between the Eucharist and common bread, but when they mentioned the age at which children have reason enough to do this they usually declared that it came between the tenth and fourteenth year of their life.

The Council of Albi (1850) declared that the age of discretion usually became the tenth and the fourteenth year.[24] At the Provincial Council of Cologne (1860) the Fathers warned that the age for admission to Holy Communion should not be confounded with the age for leaving school.[25]

The I Plenary Council of Sydney, Australia (1885), made no mention of the age at which children should first receive. It ruled that pastors or their assistants should instruct those who wished to make their first Holy Communion on the nature, efficacy and effects of the Eucharist and the dispositions required for It's worthy reception.[26]

In the United States the same tendency to set the age of discretion between the tenth and thirteenth year may be observed. The I Synod of Baltimore, convoked by Bishop Carroll (1735-1815) in 1791, decreed that pastors should not unduly defer the first Holy Communion of children, nor allow them to receive It immediately after attaining the use of reason.[27] Archbishop Kenrick (1797-1863)

[24] Decr. 5—Mansi, XLIII, 43.

[25] Cap. 23—Mansi, XLVIII, 153.

[26] C. 121—*Acta et Decreta Concilii Plenarii Australasiae Habiti apud Sydney A. D. 1885, a Sancta Sede Recognita* (Sydney: Cunningham, 1887), p. 40.

[27] C. 10—*Acta et Decreta Sacrorum Conciliorum Recentiorum, Collectio Lacensis*, Auctoribus Presbyteris S. J. e domo B. V. M. sine Labe Conceptae ad Lacum (7 vols., Friburgi Brisgoviae, 1870-1890), III, 3-4. (Hereafter cited *Coll. Lac.*).

in his *Moral Theology* taught that children usually reached the age of discretion at their twelfth year.[28]

The Fathers of the II Plenary Council of Baltimore (1866) left the judgment regarding the child's mental capacity and fitness of knowledge to those in charge of souls. The opinion of St. Thomas concerning the degree of the use of reason necessary for the reception of Holy Communion is quoted, and afterwards the general rule, which however was not absolute, was stated, namely, that the proper age is between the tenth and fourteenth year.[29]

A statute of the II Diocesan Synod of Richmond (1886) declared that children should never be admitted immediately after attaining the use of reason. Usually they could be regarded as having a sufficient maturity of judgment about their tenth year.[30] In 1909 the I Diocesan Synod of Little Rock ruled that children should be admitted between their twelfth and fourteenth year.[31] The Synod further decreed that it was the sole prerogative of chaplains of schools run by sisters to judge the fitness of pupils attending those schools, and that the exclusive judgment of the Sisters could not be accepted.[32]

The Plenary Council of Latin America held in Rome in 1899 declared that the best judges of the age at which children should be admitted to Holy Communion are the father and the confessor.[33]

Despite the teachings of many theologians and the decrees of various local councils and synods the official teaching of the Church from the thirteenth century has been that children should begin to receive Holy Communion immediately after attaining the use of reason. An examination of her legislation shows this.

Reference has already been made to the decrees of the IV Gen-

[28] *Theologia Moralis* (3 vols., Mechliniae: Dessain, 1861), II, 140.

[29] N. 261—*Coll. Lac.*, III, 3-4.

[30] N. 70—*Acta et Statuta Synodi Richmondensis Secundae* (Baltimore: John Murphy, 1886), p. 32.

[31] C. 122—*Synodus Dioecesana Petriunculana Prima* (Petriunculae: apud Cancellariam Dioecesanam, 1909), p. 59.

[32] C. 126—*Op. cit.*, p. 60.

[33] C. 528—*Acta et Decreta Concilii Plenarii Americae Latinae in Urbe Celebrati* (Romae: Typis Vaticanis, 1900), p. 230.

eral Council of the Lateran (1215),[34] and of the Council of Trent (1545-1563).[35] The Catechism of the Council of Trent states that no one can better judge the age at which a child should receive its first Holy Communion than the father and the confessor. To them it pertains to find out if the child has acquired any knowledge of and taste for this sacrament.[36]

A Council held in Rome (1725) under Benedict XIII (1724-1730) declared that children have reached the age of discretion when they can distinguish this sacramental food from common bread and know how to approach with due piety.[34]

In revising the decrees of the Provincial Council of Rouen (1850), the Sacred Congregation of the Council ordered that a canon declaring that children should not be admitted to first Holy Communion until they had attained their twelfth year be amended to read that they should not be admitted until they had acquired a knowledge of and a taste for the sacrament in the judgment especially of the pastor and the confessor.[38]

In 1884 the Bishop of Annecy in a pastoral letter made a ruling that the completion of the twelfth year and attendance at catechism classes for the two preceding years were necessary conditions for the reception of first Holy Communion. The Bishop's object in making these rules was to keep children longer in schools, and thus assure them of a more solid grounding in Catholic teaching. The decree was brought to the attention of Rome by a pastor of the diocese. The Sacred Congregation of the Council declared that these conditions bound only with regard to the public and solemn reception

[34] *Supra*, p. 10.

[35] *Supra*, p. 13.

[36] Pars II, *De Eucharistiae Sacramento*, n. 63: "Qua vero aetate pueris sacra mysteria danda sint, nemo melius constituere poterit, quam pater et sacerdos, cui illi confitentur peccata; ad illos enim pertinet explorare, et a pueris percunctari, an huius admirabilis sacramenti cognitionem aliquam acceperint, et gustum habeant."—*Catechismus ex decreto Concilii Tridentini ad parochos Pii V. Pontificis Max. et deinde Clementis XIII. iussu editus* (ed. stereotypa, Taurini-Romae: Marietti, 1930), p. 226 (hereafter cited *Catechismus Concilii Tridentini*).

[37] Appendix XXX, pars 5—*Coll. Lac.*, I, 463.

[38] *Thesaurus Resolutionum Sacrae Congregationis Concilii* (167 vols., Romae, 1718-1908), CXLVII (1888), 478 (hereafter cited *Thesaurus*).

of first Holy Communion: the Bishop was not to prohibit pastors from admitting children who had certainly reached the age of discretion according to the decrees of the IV Lateran Council and the Council of Trent.[39]

From the foregoing it is clear that Rome regarded children as having reached the age of discretion when they could distinguish the Blessed Eucharist from common bread: that the opinions of those who demanded a more advanced age were not in accordance with the mind of the Church: and that, finally, in no official pronouncement or decree can there be found any basis for distinguishing between the age for the reception of sacramental absolution and the age for the reception of Holy Communion.

Section 2. The Decree Quam Singulari

On August 8, 1910, the Sacred Congregation of the Sacraments issued the decree *Quam singulari,* the most important piece of legislation which, dealing with the communion of children, has been issued since the Council of Trent. This decree, issued with the specific approval of Pope Pius X, "The Pope of the Eucharist," was calculated to extirpate abuses with regard to the reception of the Eucharist by children, and to furnish a clear and certain rule for their future admission to the Holy Table.

The decree referred to the ancient practice of communicating children at the time of baptism. The legislation of the IV General Council of the Lateran (1215) and of the Council of Trent (1545-1563) was discussed, and the decree furthermore declared that St. Thomas (+1274), St. Antoninus (+1459), Vasquez (+1604) and Peter Ledesma (+1616) interpreted the legislation of the Lateran Council correctly. Among the errors and abuses which the decree condemned was the opinion of those who distinguished the age for the reception of First Holy Communion from the age for the reception of sacramental absolution. The error of the Jansenists in demanding an extraordinary preparation for the reception of the Eucharist was shown to conflict with the teachings of the Council of Trent.[40]

[39] *Thesaurus,* CXLVII (1888), 474-487. Cf. *Le Canoniste Contemporain* (Paris: P. Lithcilleux, 1878-1922), XII (1889), 154.

[40] *AAS,* II (1910), 580; *Fontes,* n. 2103.

The doctrine of the Angelic Doctor regarding the age of discretion was substantially adopted and given the force of law by the decree. Children were to be admitted to the reception of Holy Communion when they could distinguish the Eucharistic Bread from common and material bread, and could approach the altar in a devout manner. A perfect knowledge of the matters of faith was by no means required; a simple knowledge of the substantial elements was sufficient. It was not necessary that a child enjoy the full use of reason as a prerequisite to being admitted to the altar.[41]

The decree then gave more detailed norms to determine precisely how the age of discretion should be judged. The age of discretion was the age at which a child began to reason, that is, about the seventh year.[42] A full and perfect knowledge of Christian doctrine was not necessary for admission to first confession and Holy Communion. It sufficed if a child understood according to its capacity the mysteries necessary for salvation *necessitate medii,* could distinguish the Eucharist from common bread, and could approach the altar with a devotion becoming its age.[43]

In an article which appeared shortly after the promulgation of the decree, McNicholas discussed the amount of knowledge necessary in a candidate for first Holy Communion. The candidate had to know something about God as a supernatural Being, and something about the supernatural end of man. He had also to know that

[41] "Ex quibus omnibus colligitur aetatem discretionis ad Communionem eam esse, in qua puer panem eucharisticum a pane communi et corporali distinguere sciat ut ad altare possit devote accedere. Itaque non perfecta rerum Fidei cognitio requiritur, quum aliqua dumtaxat elementa sint satis, hoc est *aliqua cognitio;* neque plenus rationis usus, quum sufficiat usus quidam incipiens, hoc est *aliqualis usus rationis. . . .*"—*AAS,* II (1910), 581; *Fontes,* n. 2103.

[42] N. I: "Aetas discretionis tum ad Confessionem tum ad S. Communionem ea est, in qua puer incipit ratiocinari, hoc est circa septimum annum, sive supra, sive etiam infra. Ex hoc tempore incipit obligatio satisfaciendi utrique praecepto Confessionis et Communionis."—*AAS,* II (1910), 582: *Fontes,* n. 2103.

[43] N. III: "Cognitio religionis quae in puero requiritur, ut ipse ad primam Communionem convenienter se praeparet, ea est, qua ipse fidei mysteria necessaria necessitate medii pro suo captu percipiat, atque eucharisticum panem a communi et corporali distinguat ut ea devotione quam ipsius fert aetas ad SS. Eucharistiam accedat."—*loc. cit.*

God is the rewarder of the good and a punisher of the wicked. Most probably he likewise had to know something about the Blessed Trinity and the Incarnation.[44]

The obligation to ensure compliance with the precept of confession and Holy Communion by which children were bound fell upon those under whose care the children were, that is, on the parents, on the confessor, on the teachers and on the pastor.[45] Parents were bound by a natural obligation to see to it that their children approached the altar in due time. Teachers or others who had the care of the child participated in a delegated right and duty in this respect, to be exercised in the name of and by the authority of the fathers. A confessor, if the occasion arose, was bound to dispose for the immediate reception of the Eucharist a penitent who had not yet made his first Holy Communion. Finally, the pastor, as the spiritual father of the child, had the duty to see to it that when children reached the age of discretion they would go to confession and receive Holy Communion.[46]

All the foregoing regulations touched on the duty of those upon whom it was incumbent to see to it that children, when suitably qualified, fulfilled their spiritual obligations. A further and distinct question was: within whose right was it to admit children to Holy Communion? The decree *Quam singulari* declared that this right belonged to the father, or to the person taking his place, and to the confessor. It made no mention of the pastor as having any right in this regard.[47] The Roman Catechism stated that no one was better qualified to judge whether a child should be admitted to first

[44] "The Age of Children for First Communion"—*The American Ecclesiastical Review* (Philadelphia, 1889-1943; Washington, D. C., 1944—), XLIII (1910), 485 (hereafter cited *AER*).

[45] N. IV: "Obligatio praecepti Confessionis et Communionis, quae puerum gravat, in eos praecipue recidit qui curam habere debent, hoc est in parentes, in confessarium, in institutores et in parochum. . . ."—*loc. cit.*

[46] Cappello, *De aetate admittendorum ad primam Communionem Eucharisticam*, pp. 42-43.

[47] N. IV: "Ad patrem vero, aut ad illos qui vices eius gerunt, et ad confessarium, secundum Catechismum Romanum pertinet admittere puerum ad primam Communionem."—*AAS*, II (1910), 582; *Fontes*, n. 2103.

Holy Communion than the father and the confessor.[48] The pastor, then, most certainly had no exclusive right to admit children to first Holy Communion, as some had maintained.[49] So far as first Holy Communion strictly so-called was concerned, the pastor's function was to co-operate with others in seeing that children fulfilled their obligation. As for excluding those who were qualified to receive, or opposing the parents' or confessor's decision, the pastor had no rights whatsoever.[50]

It was not necessary that both the parents and the confessor agreed regarding a child's capacity to receive. Both were entitled to admit the child, so that the consent of either sufficed.[51] It was, of course, desirable that the parents and the confessor should act together in admitting a child to Holy Communion. But in the case of disagreement it seemed that either of the two could exercise complete right.[52]

The decree required pastors to arrange a General Communion of children at least once a year, and gave them the right to admit children to this Communion.[53]

Article 2. Abnormal Persons

It is generally agreed that persons who have never enjoyed the use of reason, that is, those who have never gained their reason since

[48] Cf. *supra*, p. 30, for pertinent text of the Roman Catechism.

[49] Cf. Cappello, *op. cit.*, pp. 43-44.

[50] O'Donnell, "The Decree *'Quam singulari'*—Has the Parish Priest, as such, the right to admit to First Holy Communion"—*Irish Ecclesiastical Record* (Dublin, 1864—), 5. series, II (1913), 522 (hereafter cited *IER*).

[51] O'Donnell, "The Admission of Children to Holy Communion"—*IER*, 5. series, III (1914), 82; Vermeersch, "De Primae Communionis Aetate"—*Periodica de Re Canonica et Morali utili praesertim Religiosis et Missionariis* (Brugis, 1905—), V (1913), 176 (hereafter cited *Periodica*).

[52] Zulueta, "The Control of Childrens' First Communions"—*AER*, XLVIII (1913), 24.

[53] N. V: "Semel aut pluries in anno curent parochi indicere atque habere Communionem generalem puerorum, ad eamque non modo novensiles admittere, sed etiam alios, qui parentum confessariive consensu, ut supra dictum est, iam antea primitus de altari sancta libarunt. . . ."—*AAS*, II (1910), 582; *Fontes*, n. 2103.

birth, should not be allowed to receive Holy Communion. Thus, Suarez stated that such persons, since they are incapable of the devotion with which the Sacrament should be approached, should not be allowed to receive.[54] The rule of the Roman Ritual of Pope Paul V (1605-1621) stated clearly that it is not allowable to communicate such persons.[55] From that time onward authors merely stated the fact that it was unlawful to communicate those who were perpetually insane, citing the rubric of the *Roman Ritual*.[56]

Opinion was divided on the point whether one not always insane could receive Holy Communion *in articulo mortis,* when at the time of death he has not enjoyed the use of reason for some time past. Those who held that such a person could receive, provided that there was no danger of irreverence to the Host, followed the opinion of St. Thomas.[57]

Suarez (1548-1617) taught that in such circumstances an insane person could receive.[58] De Lugo (1583-1660) argued that, if the dying insane person had manifested his intention of receiving some time beforehand, there was no reason why Viaticum should not be

[54] *De Sacramento Eucharistiae,* q. 80, art. 9, disp. 68, sec. 6—*Opera Omnia,* XXI, 520.

[55] Tit. 4, c. 1, *de Sacramento Eucharistiae,* n. 10—"Amentibus praeterea, seu phreneticis communicare non licet: licebit tamen, si quando habeant lucida intervalla, et devotionem ostendant, dum in eo statu manent, si nullum indignitatis periculum adsit."—*Rituale Romanum, Pauli V Maximi iussu editum, et a Benedicto XIV Auctum et Castigatum* (Baltimore: John Murphy, 1873), p. 108. The present *Roman Ritual* (New York: Benziger, 1925) retains this ruling in identical words. Cf. tit. IV, c. 1, *de Sanctissimo Eucharistiae Sacramento,* n. 10, as contained on p. 86.

[56] Liguori, *Theologia Moralis,* Lib. VI, *de Eucharistia,* n. 302; Gasparri, *Tractatus Canonicus de Sanctissima Eucharistia* (2 vols., Parisiis: Delhomme et Briguet, 1897), II, n. 1123, p. 356 (hereafter cited *De Sanctissima Eucharistia*); Noldin, *Summa Theologiae Moralis* (5. ed., 3 vols., Oeniponte: Rauch, 1904), III, n. 138, p. 153; Genicot, *Theologiae Moralis Institutiones* (6. ed., 2 vols., Bruxellis: Dewit, 1909), II, n. 190, p. 182.

[57] *Summa Theologica,* Pars III, q. 80, a. 9: "Si prius, quando erant compotes suae mentis, apparuit in eis devotio huius sacramenti, debet eis in articulo mortis hoc sacramentum exhiberi, nisi forte timeatur periculum vomitus, vel exspuitionis." Cf. also *ibid.,* ad 3.

[58] *De Sacramento Eucharistiae,* q. 80, art. 9, disp. 68, sec. 6—*Opera Omnia,* XXI, 520.

given, just as extreme unction was given.[59] The Catechism of the Council of Trent likewise had allowed persons of this class to receive at the time of death.[60]

St. Alphonsus (1696-1787) asserted that an interpretative intention to receive could be presumed to exist in such a case. He argued that the Eucharist may even be necessary, namely, if the person became bereft of his reason while he was in the state of mortal sin for which he had conceived only an act of attrition.[61]

Gasparri (1852-1934) seemed to favor the view that the rule of the *Roman Ritual*[62] was absolute and that, in consequence, the Eucharist should not be given to an actually insane person *in articulo mortis* even if the previously expressed intention to receive still habitually existed. However, he refrained from condemning those who held that Viaticum could be administered to such a person.[63]

Genicot (1856-1900), after referring to both opinions, concluded that in practice it was best not to administer Holy Communion, lest the Sacred Species be exposed to the danger of irreverence.[64] Noldin (1838-1922) suggested that the priest could give the patient an unconsecrated host to see if there was any danger of irreverence.[65]

During lucid intervals, as long as the other essential conditions are present, there is nothing to prevent a habitually insane man from receiving the Blessed Eucharist if there is no danger of irreverence. The *Roman Ritual* teaches this,[66] and authors gener-

[59] *De Sacramento Eucharistiae*, disp. 13, sect. 3, n. 24—*Disputationes Scholasticae et Moralis*, IV, 59.

[60] Pars II, *De Eucharistiae Sacramento*, n. 64—"Quamvis si antequam in insaniam inciderent, piam et religiosam animi voluntatem praesetulerunt, licebit eis in fine vitae, ex concilii Carthaginiensis decreto, Eucharistiam administrare, modo vomitionis, vel alterius indignitatis et incommodi periculum nullum timendum sit."—*Catechismus Concilii Tridentini*, p. 226.

[61] *Theologia Moralis*, Lib. VI, *de Eucharistia*, n. 302.

[62] Cf. *supra*, footnote 55, for the text of the Ritual.

[63] *De Sanctissima Eucharistia*, II, pp. 357-358, n. 1124.

[64] *Theologiae Moralis Institutiones*, II, p. 183, n. 190.

[65] *Summa Theologiae Moralis*, III, p. 155, n. 139.

[66] Cf. *supra*, p. 25, footnote 55.

ally are satisfied simply to cite the rubric of the *Roman Ritual* in support of their statement that Holy Communion may then be administered.[67]

Those who have the use of reason in but a feeble and vapid manner (*semifatui*) can receive if they are able to distinguish between the sacrament and common bread, and have a perceptive taste and appreciation for the sacrament. Suarez,[68] Liguori,[69] Gasparri,[70] Gury (1801-1866)-Ballerini (1805-1881),[71] and Noldin,[72] are all agreed on this. All likewise agreed that such persons can receive at the time of death and at Paschal time. Noldin readily allowed them to receive more often according to the greater or lesser amount of discretion they enjoyed,[73] and Genicot indicated that the confessor was to be the judge.[74]

According to Liguori Holy Communion was to be altogether refused to those who were born blind, deaf and dumb.[75] Gasparri, agreeing with this opinion remarked that Holy Communion was not to be given to them even if they were instructed.[76]

The test of the lawfulness of communicating those who without being blind are at the same time deaf and dumb is the amount of discretion they possess. Liguori allowed them to receive Holy Communion at least at Paschal time and in proximate danger of death.[77]

67 Genicot, *loc. cit.;* Gasparri, *loc. cit.;* Gury-Ballerini, *Compendium Theologiae Moralis* (9 ed., 2 vols., Romae: ex Typographia Polyglotta, 1887), II, 216-217.

68 *De Sacramento Eucharistiae,* q. 80, n. 3—*Opera Omnia,* XXI, 520.

69 *Theologia Moralis,* Lib. VI, *de Eucharistia,* n. 303.

70 *Op. cit.,* II, n. 1123, p. 356.

71 *Op. cit.,* II, *loc. cit.*

72 *Op. cit.,* III, n. 139, p. 155.

73 *Loc. cit.*

74 *Loc. cit.*

75 *Theologia Moralis,* Lib. VI, *de. Eucharistia,* n. 303.

76 *Loc. cit.;* cf. Cappello, *Tractatus Canonico-Moralis de Sacramentis* (3 vols. in 6, Vol. I, 4. ed., 1945, Romae: Marietti), I, 366 (hereafter cited *De Sacramentis*).

77 *Loc. cit.*

Gury-Ballerini,[78] Gasparri [79] and Genicot [80] likewise subscribed to this doctrine, demanding simply a sufficient use of reason and instruction.

Article 3. First Holy Communion as Viaticum

Section 1. When Viaticum can be Given

The great majority of theologians held that the precept of receiving Holy Communion *in articulo mortis* is a precept of divine origin. Vasquez defended this view [81] and Suarez called the opinion probable.[82] De Lugo defended this same view against Bonaventure (1221-1274), Silvester Prieras (1456-1523) and Armilla (Bartholomaeus Fumus +1545).[83] St. Alphonsus,[84] Gury-Ballerini,[85] Genicot [86] and Noldin [87] also held that the precept to receive *in articulo mortis* is of divine law.

Theologians interpreted the phrase *in articulo mortis* as any proximate danger of death, whether it arise from an intrinsic or an extrinsic cause. Thus St. Alphonsus taught that in any imminent mortal danger to life which one foresaw, or with good reason feared, there was a grave obligation to communicate.[88] Genicot stated that the precept obliges in proximate danger of death, no matter from what cause this danger arises.[89] Gasparri asserted that it is a matter of indifference whether the danger arises from an intrinsic cause, such as from a disease, or from an extrinsic cause, such as a capital sentence.[90]

[78] *Op. cit.,* II, 219.

[79] *Loc. cit.*

[80] *Loc. cit.*

[81] *Libri Commentariorum in Tertiam Partem S. Thomae* disp. 214, cap. 2, nn. 6-10, III, 344.

[82] *De Eucharistia,* q. 71, art. II, disp. 69, sec. 3, n. 2—*Opera Omnia* XXI, 533.

[83] *De Sacramento Eucharistiae,* disp. 16, sec. 2, n. 27—*op. cit.,* IV, 140.

[84] *Theologia Moralis,* Lib. VI, *de Eucharistia,* n. 290.

[85] *Compendium Theologiae Moralis,* II, 209.

[86] *Theologiae Moralis Institutiones,* II, 198.

[87] *Summa Theologiae Moralis,* III, n. 139, p. 156.

[88] *Theologia Moralis,* Lib. VI, *de Eucharistia,* n. 291.

[89] *Theologiae Moralis Institutiones,* II, n. 206, p. 198.

[90] *De Sanctissima Eucharistia,* II, n. 1147, pp. 372-373.

Perhaps the most comprehensive definition of the meaning of the phrase *periculum mortis* was given by D'Annibale (1815-1892), who spoke of it as:

> . . . illud rerum discrimen, in quo cum quis constitutus est, ipsum, et superesse, et occumbere posse, utrumque est vere graviterque probabile; sive periculum immineat *ab intrinseco,* ut puta ex morbo, vulnere inflicto, partu difficili, extrema senectute; sive *ab extrinseco* immineat, velut ex bello, navigatione periculosa, etc. Hoc amplius: si quis versetur in periculo incidendi in perpetuam amentiam, perinde habetur ac si versaretur in periculo mortis.[91]

Two responses of the Sacred Congregation for the Propagation of the Faith confirm the fact that the danger of death which urges the obligation of receiving Holy Communion may derive either from an intrinsic or from an extrinsic source. The first, dated February 20, 1801, was an affirmative answer to the question whether missioners in China could give Viaticum and extreme unction to persons suffering from tuberculosis or from some other disease, when it was foreseen that they would linger on for many months, but when it was likewise foreseen that they would certainly die within a year and at a time when missioners could not attend to administer these sacraments to them in consequence of their removal at a great distance or from some other hindering circumstances.[92]

The second reply dealt with prisoners condemned to death. A question which was submitted to the Sacred Congregation asked if Holy Communion could be brought to priests and Christians condemned to death for the faith on the day of, or on the day preceding, their execution. The answer given was: "In the affirmative, and by way of Viaticum." A second question submitted at the same time asked if Holy Communion could be brought to those justly or unjustly condemned to death or perpetual imprisonment if they had received absolution, especially if they asked for Holy Communion. The answer was: "In the affirmative and *ad mentem,* namely, that

[91] *Summula Theologiae Moralis* (4. ed., 3 vols., Romae, Ex Typographia Polyglotta, 1894), I, n. 38.

[92] *Fontes,* n. 4662; *Collect.,* n. 651.

the Vicar Apostolic should take extreme care that those condemned to death be nourished with this heavenly bread.[93] Finally, an Instruction of the same Congregation ordered that all the dying among the poor be given Viaticum.[94] The essential difference between simple Holy Communion and Communion by way of Viaticum lies in the different formulas prescribed in the *Roman Ritual* for the administration of each. The formula for simple Holy Communion is:

> Corpus Domini nostri Jesu Christi custodiat animam tuam in vitam aeternam. Amen.[95]

The formula to be used in the administration of Viaticum reads:

> Accipe, frater (*vel* soror) Viaticum Corporis Domini nostri Jesu Christi, qui te custodiat ab hoste maligno, et perducat in vitam aeternam. Amen.[96]

Vazquez stated that the reception of Holy Communion in the form of Viaticum does not depend on the will of the subject. Holy Communion is to be received as Viaticum when the precept to receive *in articulo mortis* obliges.[97] The *Roman Ritual* rules that Communion shall be administered as Viaticum when it is probable that the subject will have no further opportunity for receiving.[98] Gasparri concluded that it is necessary, but that it also suffices, for the administration of Holy Communion as Viaticum that the subject be in danger of death.[99]

From the cited responses of the Sacred Congregation for the Propagation of the Faith,[100] and from the wording of the *Roman*

[93] S. C. de Prop. Fide (C. P. pro Sin.—Tunkin Occident.), 21 iul. 1841, ad 1 et 2—*Fontes*, n. 4789; *Collect.*, n. 928.

[94] S. C. de Prop. Fide, instr. 31 iul., 1902, n. 6—*Fontes*, n. 4940; *Collect.*, n. 2149.

[95] *Rituale Romanum*, tit. IV, cap. 2, *de sanctissimo Eucharistiae Sacramento.*

[96] *Rituale Romanum*, tit. IV, cap. 4, *de communione infirmorum.*

[97] *Libri Commentariorum in Tertiam Partem S. Thomae*, disp. 214, cap. 2, n. 17, III, 345.

[98] "Pro Viatico autem ministrabit, cum probabile est, quod eam amplius sumere non poterit."—tit. IV, cap. 4, *de communione infirmorum*, n. 4.

[99] *De Sanctissima Eucharistia*, II, n. 1101, p. 341.

[100] *Supra*, p. 29.

Ritual, the general rule can be drawn that Holy Communion should be administered as Viaticum when it is probable that the subject cannot again receive it. The danger of irreverence must always be guarded against in the administration of the Eucharist. The *Roman Ritual* warns that It should not be given to those from whom, on account of frenzy, or in consequence of a persistent cough, or for some similar malady, irreverence is to be feared.[101]

Gury-Ballerini asserted that a delirious patient could be permitted to receive the Eucharist if he was capable of doing so without any accompanying danger of irreverence. The giving of an unconsecrated host for exploring the possible presence of this danger was recommended.[102] Noldin stated that Holy Communion could be given to delirious people when they were in danger of death, if they enjoyed a lucid interval and if no danger of irreverence was present. He also recommended the experiment with the unconsecrated host.[103] Genicot required in addition that the sick person have lived piously, so that he could be presumed to have an interpretive intention of receiving at the time of death. In practice, however, it was safer not to give the Blessed Eucharist, lest it be exposed to the danger of irreverence.[104]

Other potential sources of irreverence are coughing and vomiting. St. Alphonsus remarked that, if the cough was so severe that the Host could not be swallowed, It should not be given. Once it has been swallowed there is no danger of irreverence to be feared from expectoration, since the phlegm does not come from the stomach.[105]

Noldin felt that irreverence was to be feared only if a fit of coughing were provoked at the actual reception, and not if it continued or arose thereafter, since the source of the sputum was not the stom-

[101] Tit. IV, cap. 4, *de communione infirmorum*, n. 5: ". . . id tamen diligenter curandum est, ne iis tribuatur, a quibus ob phrenesim, sive ob assiduam tussim, aliumve similem morbum, aliqua indecentia cum iniuria tanti Sacramenti timeri potest. . . ."

[102] *Compendium Theologiae Moralis*, II, 219.

[103] *Summa Theologiae Moralis*, III, n. 139, p. 154.

[104] *Theologiae Moralis Institutiones*, II, n. 190, p. 183.

[105] *Theologia Moralis*, Lib. VI, *de Eucharistia*, n. 292.

ach.[106] Genicot was of the opinion that only very rarely does a person suffer from a cough that makes it impossible for him to swallow the Host securely.[107]

St. Alphonsus favored the practice of giving a small particle of an unconsecrated host by way of experiment to one from whom the danger of vomiting was feared. If the sick person could not retain this, then on no account should Holy Communion be given to him. Neither should it be given to one who vomits independently of whether he has or has not received food, unless he has been free from vomiting for at least six hours.[108]

For the reception of the Eucharist Noldin required that the patient be free from vomiting for an hour after receiving an unconsecrated particle. In doubt whether the sick person would vomit, Holy Communion was not to be given.[109] According to Genicot only a doctor is capable of stating whether a sufficient time will elapse for the safe reception of Holy Communion before the patient begins to vomit again. According to the same author there is no necessity always to wait until the person has been free from vomiting for six hours.[110]

Section 2. Children as the Recipients

The common practice since the time of the Council of Trent has been to give Viaticum to dying children who have reached the use of reason, even though in the ordinary course of events they would not have been admitted to receive Holy Communion for some time.

De Lugo, following the teaching of Suarez, professed the opinion that children who when dying had reached the use of reason should be given the Eucharist.[111] Benedict XIV, after examining the opinions of various authors, concluded that a less advanced age was

[106] *Op. cit., loc. cit.*

[107] *Op. cit.*, II, n. 191, p. 183.

[108] *Theologia Moralis*, Lib. VI, *de Eucharistia*, n. 292.

[109] *Loc. cit.*

[110] *Loc. cit.*

[111] *De Sacramento Eucharistiae*, disp. 13, sec. 4, n. 37—*Disputationes Scholasticae et Morales*, IV, 63.

required for the reception of the Eucharist as Viaticum on the part of dying children. Bishops were to admonish and exhort their pastors not to let all children alike die without Holy Viaticum. Pastors were diligently to examine the dying child to see if it believed that Christ was present in the Sacred Species, so that it could reverently adore It. It was to be left to the judgment of the pastor to decide whether the dying child was a fit subject for the reception of Viaticum.[112] St. Alphonsus explained that, on the one hand, such children are bound by divine precept to communicate, and, on the other hand, the potential utility of the Eucharist when received as Viaticum does not postulate more by way of disposition than the acquired use of reason.[113]

Various local councils enacted legislation to regulate the reception of Holy Communion by children when they were dying or when they were in danger of death. In general, children who were not allowed to receive in the ordinary course of events because of the lack of the prescribed knowledge or age were nevertheless allowed to receive in danger of death.

The Council of Albi (1850) allowed such children to communicate, provided that they knew the mysteries of faith, and especially that Christ was present in the Eucharist.[114] Similar legislation had been made in the Council of Soissons in the year 1849. In it the Fathers decreed that the Eucharist should not be denied to dying children even though they had not yet reached the prescribed age.[115]

[112] "Quare nulli controversae opinioni calculum adiicit Episcopus, qui in sua Synodo Parochos serio adhortatur, et monet, ne patiantur, omnes pueros indiscriminatim interire sine Christi Corporis Viatico, illudque iis praebendum praecipit, quos iidem Parochi, diligenti praemisso examine, tanta compererint pollere perspicacia, ut latentem sub specibus sacramentalibus Christum et firmiter credant, et reverenter adorent: . . . ipsiusmet prudentis Parochi iudicio permittitur definire, an moriturus puer, spectata eius indole, sit tanti Sacramenti capax."—*De Synodo Dioecesana* (4 vols., Mechliniae, 1842), Lib. VII, cap. 12, n. 3.

[113] *Theologia Moralis*, Lib. VI, *de Eucharistia*, n. 301.

[114] Can. 7: ". . . pueris quoque nondum ad sacram synaxim admissis, modo mysteria fidei, et imprimis Christum in eucharistia praesentem, noverint."—Mansi, LXIII, 932.

[115] Can. 3: "Non deneganda est imo potius conferenda pueris, qui primae communionis aetatem nondum adepti, ad usum tamen rationis pervenerunt,

A reply of the Holy Office given in 1861 stated that Viaticum should not be given to dying adult neophytes unless they could distinguish the spiritual from the material food, and actually recognized and believed in the presence of Christ in the Sacred Host.[116]

The II Plenary Council of Baltimore (1866) reminded priests that *in articulo mortis* a less mature age was required for the communion of children, provided only that they could distinguish the Eucharist from common bread.[117]

Genicot taught that Viaticum should regularly be given to children in danger of death if they have completed their seventh year and have some knowledge of the sacrament. If there be doubt that the child has reached the age of discretion, the pastor has no obligation of giving Viaticum, but is free to take whatever course he thinks will profit the child most.[118]

The decree *Quam singulari* regarded the practice which allowed children who had reached the use of reason to die without Viaticum as an utterly detestable abuse, and decreed that the ordinary was to proceed severely against those who did not abandon that practice.[119]

modo edocti, prout tempus permiserit, cibum coelestem et supernum a communi et materiali discernere queant."—Mansi, XLIII, 587.

[116] S. C. S. Off. (Tchely Meridio-Oriental), 10 apr. 1861 ad 1: "Praeterea hisce neophytis moribundis non esse administrandum Viaticum nisi saltem discernant cibum spiritualem a corporali, cognoscendo et credendo in Sacra Hostia praesentiam Christi Domini."—*Fontes*, n. 965.

[117] N. 261: "Meminerint vero sacerdotes tantam non desiderari aetatem, ut quis in articulo mortis Sanctissimo Viatico possit et debeat muniri. . . . Si qui igitur 'pueri nondum satis edocti periculose decumbant, eos Divini hujus Mysterii notitia imbuere studeant, neque dubitent illis Divinum hunc Cibum praebere, si Divinum Panem satis a vulgari descernere didicerint, atque aliquo erga illum pietatis sensu affici cognoverint.'"—*Coll. Lac.*, III, 467.

[118] *Theologiae Moralis Institutiones*, II, n. 211, p. 203.

[119] N. VIII: "Detestabilis omnino est abusus non ministrandi Viaticum et Extremum Unctionem pueris post usum rationis eosque sepeliendi ritu parvulorum. In eos, qui ab huiusmodi more non recedant, Ordinarii locorum severe animadvertant."—*AAS*, II (1910), 583; *Fontes*, n. 2103.

PART TWO

CANONICAL COMMENTARY

CHAPTER III

THE OBLIGATION TO RECEIVE HOLY COMMUNION

ARTICLE 1. THE NATURE OF THE OBLIGATION AND THE MANNER OF FULFILLMENT

Section 1. The Nature of the Obligation

Can. 859, § 1. Omnis utriusque sexus fidelis, postquam ad annos discretionis, idest ad rationis usum, pervenerit, debet semel in anno, saltem in Paschate, Eucharistiae sacramentum recipere, nisi forte de consilio proprii sacerdotis, ob aliquam rationabilem causam, ad tempus ab eius perceptione duxerit abstinendum.[1]

It is clear from the words of Christ, "Amen, Amen, I say to you, unless you eat the flesh of the Son of Man, and drink his blood, you shall not have life in you," [2] that there is a divine positive precept to receive Holy Communion. Theologians and canonists infer from these words that in simple consequence of the command inherent in them (*per se*) the obligation to receive Holy Communion binds the faithful who have reached the use of reason to approach the altar several times during life as well as in danger of death, and that in consequence of incidental reasons (*per accidens*), such as the consideration of vanquishing an otherwise insurmountable

[1] *Codex Iuris Canonici Pii X Pontificis Maximi iussu digestus Benedicti Papae XV auctoritate promulgatus* (Romae: Typis Polyglottis Vaticanis, 1917).

[2] John, VI: 54.

temptation, that same obligation calls for fulfillment whenever such reasons urge it.[3] Christ did not determine the precise number of times men were bound to approach the altar during life, but implicitly gave His Church the power to do so by giving her the power to dispense the sacraments. In virtue of this power the Church has determined the number of times outside the danger of death that men must receive Holy Communion in order to fulfill the divine precept.

The fervor of the early Christians led them to communicate frequently, and hence there was no need of positive legislation to indicate their obligation for them. But when the devotion of the faithful began to grow cold, it became necessary to determine the obligation of receiving the Eucharist at certain times. Thus the Council of Agde (506) [4] and the Council of Tours (813) [5] required the faithful to receive Holy Communion at least three times each year. The first general determination of the divine law is to be found in the legislation of the IV General Council of the Lateran (1215). Its law, expressed in the famous decree *Omnis utriusque,* required all the faithful of both sexes who had reached the age of discretion to receive Holy Communion during the Paschal season.[6] This law was confirmed by the legislation of the Council of Trent (1545-1563).[7] The legislation of the IV Lateran Council on this point is now incorporated among the canons of the Code of Canon Law.[8]

From what has been said it is obvious that the law which re-

[3] Gasparri, *De Sanctissima Eucharistia,* II, pp. 372-373, n. 1146-1147; Cappello, *De Sacramentis,* I, 385-387; Prümmer, *Manuale Theologiae Moralis* (3 vols., Vol. I, 8. ed., Vol. II, 4. et 5. ed., Vol. III, 6. et 7. ed., Friburgi-Brisgoviae: Herder, 1928-1935), III, 155; Merkelbach, *Summa Theologiae Moralis* (3. ed., 3 vols., Desclée, 1939), III, 242; Sabetti-Barrett, *Compendium Theologiae Moralis* (27 ed., New York: Pustet, 1919), p. 628; Tanquerey, *Synopsis Theologiae Dogmaticae,* III, 648-649.

[4] C. 18—Mansi, VIII, 327; Bruns, *Canones Apostolorum et conciliorum saeculorum IV-VII* (2 vols., Berolini: Reimeri, 1839), II, 50.

[5] C. 50—Mansi, XIV, 91.

[6] Cf. *supra*, p. 10, for a discussion of the pertinent canon.

[7] Sess. XIII, *de Eucharistia,* can. 9—Schroeder, *Canons and Decrees of the Council of Trent,* p. 356.

[8] Canon 859, § 1.

quires the faithful to communicate during the Paschal season each year is partly a divine law and partly an ecclesiastical law. It imports a double obligation: the primary and principal obligation of communicating each year, and the secondary obligation of communicating within the Paschal season. Insofar as the enactment implies a determination by the Church of the obligation of the divine law to receive Holy Communion several times during life, the law contained in canon 859, § 1, is a divine-ecclesiastical law. Insofar as the Church requires the faithful to fulfill this obligation during the Paschal season, the law contained in canon 859, § 1, is purely (*mere*) an ecclesiastical law.

One reception of Holy Communion during the Paschal season suffices to satisfy both the divine-ecclesiastical and the purely ecclesiastical law. Both of those obligations are grave, and consequently any deliberate neglect in the fulfilling of either would result in the commission of a mortal sin. Of the two, however, the divine-ecclesiastical obligation is the more grave. Should one fail to fulfill the purely ecclesiastical law by not receiving the Eucharist during the Paschal season, the divine-ecclesiastical obligation of receiving annually still binds under pain of grave sin.

Section 2. The Manner of Fulfilling the Obligation.

Can. 859, § 2. Paschalis communio fiat a dominica Palmarum ad dominicam in albis; sed locorum Ordinariis fas est, si ita personarum ac locorum adiuncta exigant, hoc tempus etiam pro omnibus suis fidelibus anticipare, non tamen ante quartam diem dominicam Quadragesimae, vel prorogare, non ultra festum sanctissimae Trinitatis.

Can. 861. Praecepto communionis recipiendae non satisfit per sacrilegam communionem.

Canon 859, § 1, declares that the season for the fulfilling of the purely ecclesiastical precept extends from Palm Sunday to Low Sunday. The same canon gives local ordinaries the power to extend this period from the Fourth Sunday in Lent to Trinity Sunday if this extension is warranted by personal or local conditions.[9] In the United States, in virtue of an apostolic indult, local ordinaries can further extend the Paschal season from the First Sunday in Lent to Trinity Sunday.[10] The Paschal season is determined in such fashion that the reception of Holy Communion on the day before the season begins or on the day after it expires does not satisfy the purely ecclesiastical precept.

Reference has already been made to the divine-ecclesiastical precept of communicating annually. The question now arises: How is this year to be computed? Some canonists insist that the year is to be calculated according to the civil calendar, that is, from January 1 to December 31 inclusive.[11] Other canonists assert that the year during which the divine-ecclesiastical obligation must be fulfilled covers that span of time which elapses between the beginning of one Paschal season and the beginning of the following.[12] This latter view seems to be the more acceptable one, since it is based on the teaching and interpretation furnished by Pope Eugene IV

[9] Cf. canon 198, §§ 1-2, for a list of persons who in law come under the name "local ordinary."

[10] This indult, issued by the Congregation for the Propagation of the Faith on October 16, 1830, is referred to in n. 257 of the II Plenary Council of Baltimore (1866). The indult was granted in consideration of a petition presented to the Holy See by the bishops assembled in the I Provincial Council of Baltimore (1829). The wording both of the presented petition and of the granted indult is reported in the *Coll. Lac.*, III, 35-36.

The indult may still be used, since it is not revoked by the canons of the Code. According to canon 4, indults issued by the Apostolic See which are still in use (i.e. at the time of the promulgation of the Code), and not revoked, remain intact unless they are expressly revoked by the canons of the Code.—Cf. Murphy, "General Norms of Canon Law as found in the First Book of the Code"—*The Jurist* (Washington, D. C.: The Catholic University of America, 1941—), IV (1944), 386.

[11] Vermeersch-Creusen, *Epitome Iuris Canonici* (3 vols., Vol. II, 4. ed., Mechliniae-Romae: Dessain, 1930), II, 77; Coronata, *Tractatus Canonicus de Sacramentis* (3 vols., Romae: Marietti, 1943-1945), I, 309-310.

[12] Gasparri, *De Sanctissima Eucharistia*, II, p. 378, n. 1156; Cappello, *De Sacramentis*, I, 390; Noldin-Schmitt, *Summa Theologiae Moralis iuxta Codicem Iuris Canonici* (3 vols., Vols. I, III, 23. ed., 1935, Vol. II, 22. ed., 1934, Oeniponte: Typis et Sumptibus Fel. Rauch), II, 642 (hereafter cited *Summa Theologiae Moralis*).

(1431-1447) with reference to the law of the Lateran Council.[13] However, the first viewpoint is not without some probability, since it is supported by canonists of high standing. Hence it may be safely followed. It is not legitimate to alternate between those two methods of computation during the same year in order to free oneself from the obligation imposed by the law which prescribes annual Communion.

Through a sacrilegious reception of the Eucharist one does not fulfill the obligation of receiving Holy Communion. In this respect to receive sacrilegiously is regarded as the equivalent of not receiving at all.[14]

Article 2. The Age of Discretion and the Obligation to Receive

Section 1. Children Under the Age of Discretion

Can. 854, § 1. Pueris, qui propter aetatis imbecillitatem nondum huius sacramenti cognitionem et gustum habent, Eucharistia ne ministretur.

Without any opposition to divine law, children who have not yet reached the age of discretion can fruitfully receive Holy Communion. Christ did not limit Its reception to those who enjoyed the use of reason when He issued the precept to eat His Flesh and to drink His Blood. A survey in history regarding the age at which children were admitted to Holy Communion shows that in the Latin Church from the earliest times until the twelfth century it was customary to administer the Eucharist to infants immediately after their baptism.[15] This custom still survives in certain localities in

[13] Ep. *"Fide digna,"* 8 iul. 1440, § 2: ". . . sed terminum statuisse a Pascha ad Pascham."—*Fontes,* n. 53.

[14] A proposition declaring that by means of a sacrilegious Communion one satisfied the precept of annual Communion was condemned by the Holy Office in a decree dated March 4, 1679—Denzinger, n. 1205. Cf. canon 861: "Praecepto communionis recipiendae non satisfit per sacrilegam communionem."

[15] Cf. chapter I.

the East among Greeks and Orientals in communion with Rome. On June 16, 1761, the Sacred Congregation for the Propagation of the Faith declared that the practice should not be changed.[16] The Council of Trent expressly refrained from condemning the early Latin Fathers who followed the custom, and declared that it was certain and beyond controversy that those early Fathers in no way believed that the Eucharist was necessary for the salvation of infants.[17]

Though children who have not yet reached the years of discretion are by divine law capable of fruitfully receiving Holy Communion, it by no means follows that they are bound to do so. As has been noted, the IV General Council of the Lateran (1215) imposed the obligation of receiving the Eucharist on those only who had reached the years of discretion. Since the Eucharist is not necessary for the salvation of those who are under the age of discretion,[18] the Church has wisely decided that It should not be administered to them on account of the danger of irreverence.[19]

The Code of Canon Law forbids the administration of the Eucharist to children who on account of their tender age do not possess a knowledge and an appreciation of the Sacrament.[20] Severe penalties may be inflicted on anyone who dares to communicate such a child.[21]

[16] *Collect.*, n. 713.

[17] Sess. XXI, *de Communione,* c. 4—Schroeder, *Canons and Decrees of the Council of Trent,* p. 408.

[18] *Conc. Trident.*, sess. XXI, *de Communione,* can. 4: "Si quis dixerit, parvulis, antequam ad annos discretionis pervenerint, necessariam esse Eucharistiae communionem: anathema sit."—Schroeder, *op. cit.*, p. 409.

[19] S. C. de Sacr., decr. 8 aug. 1910—*AAS,* II (1910), 577; *Fontes,* n. 2103.

[20] Cf. canon 854, § 1. Blat understands the word *imbecillitatem* as denoting a lack of the use of reason in view of the tender age of the child.—*Commentarium Textus Iuris Canonici* (5 vols. in 6, Vol. III, Pars I (*De Sacramentis*), Romae: Ex Typographia Pontificia Pii X, 1920), III, Pars I, 186 (hereafter the I part of this volume is cited *De Sacramentis*).

[21] Canon 2364. Minister qui ausus fuerit Sacramenta administrare illis qui iure sive divino sive ecclesiastico eadem recipere prohibentur, suspendatur ab administrandis Sacramentis per tempus prudenti Ordinarii arbitrio definiendum aliisque poenis pro gravitate culpae puniatur, firmis peculiaribus poenis in aliqua huius generis delicta iure statutis. These penalties are of a *ferendae sententiae*

Section 2. Children Who Have Reached the Age of Discretion.

Can. 859, § 1. Omnis utriusque sexus fidelis, postquam ad annos discretionis, idest ad rationis usum, pervenerit, debet semel in anno, saltem in Paschate, Eucharistiae sacramentum recipere, nisi forte de consilio proprii sacerdotis, ob aliquam rationabilem causam, ad tempus ab eius perceptione duxerit abstinendum.

When a child reaches the age of discretion it becomes subject to the law which requires the faithful to receive Holy Communion each year during the Paschal season. The question now arises: When does a child reach the age of discretion?

In determining the age at which a child is bound to receive the Eucharist, the Code uses the words *"postquam ad annos discretionis, idest ad rationis usum, pervenerit."* [22] From the wording of this clause it is apparent that when a child has attained the years of discretion it has also reached the use of reason. The phrase *"ad annos discrĕtionis"* has the same significance as the phrase *"ad rationis usum."* The attribution of an identical meaning to these two phrases is not an innovation in ecclesiastical legislation. According to Gasparri (1852-1934) the Fathers of the IV General Council of the Lateran (1215) used the phrase *"postquam ad annos discretionis pervenerit"* to signify the attaining of the use of reason.[23] The Council of Trent used the phrases *"usu rationis carentes"* and *"antequam ad annos discretionis pervenerint"* to designate that class of children which was not bound to receive Holy Communion.[24] Hence there is no foundation in law for a distinction between the age

nature.—Cf. Chelodi, *Ius Canonicum de Delictis et Poenis* (5. ed., Vicenza: Società Anonima Tipografica, 1943), p. 133 (hereafter cited *De Delictis et Poenis*).

[22] Canon 859, § 1.

[23] *De Sanctissima Eucharistia,* II, 386, n. 1167.

[24] Sess. XXI, *de Communione,* can. 4—Schroeder, *Canons and Decrees of the Council of Trent,* pp. 408-409.

when a child attains the years of discretion and the age when it acquires the use of reason. The present writer will use both phrases as having the same meaning.

It is impossible to determine with mathematical accuracy the age at which children in general reach the use of reason, in view of the many factors which must be taken into consideration. The mental development of the child, the maturity of its judgment, the care expended in its education, and the amount of knowledge it possesses—all these factors play a part in a child's earlier or later attainment of the age of discretion. It seems certain that children develop the use of reason more quickly at the present time than they did centuries ago. St. Thomas (1225-1274) regarded children as having enough use of reason for their admission to Holy Communion when they were about ten or eleven years old.[25] At the present time the normal child develops a sufficient use of reason for its admission to Holy Communion at a somewhat earlier age. The most the present writer can hope to do is to delineate some general rules which determine whether or not an individual child has reached the years of discretion.

It is evident that a child develops only gradually the full use of its reason. Experiments conducted by leading modern psychologists show that the ability to reason increases by small increments in proportion to age.[26] The full use of its reason is not required as a prerequisite for its admission to the Eucharist. St. Thomas taught that it was enough if children had some use of reason or had begun to reason.[27] Similarly the decree *Quam singulari* ruled that the age of discretion both for confession and Communion was that age at which children began to reason.[28] The decision as to the point of

[25] *In IV Libros Sententiarum,* dist. 9, q. 1, art. 5, solutio 4: "Pueris autem iam incipientibus habere discretionem, etiam ante perfectam aetatem, puta cum sint decem vel undecim annorum aut circa hoc, potest dari si in eis signa discretionis appareant et devotionis."—*Opera Omnia,* X, 230.

[26] Cf. Munn, *Psychological Development* (Cambridge: Riverside Press, 1938), p. 368.

[27] Cf. *supra,* p. 21.

[28] S. C. de Sacramentis, decr. 8 aug. 1910, n. I: "Aetas discretionis tum ad Confessionem tum ad S. Communionem ea est, in qua puer incipit ratiocinari, hoc est circa septimum annum, sive supra, sive etiam infra. Ex hoc tempore

time at which a child reaches the age of discretion now resolves itself into deciding when a child begins to reason. There is little use in appealing to the findings of psychologists for an answer to the question. The results of their experiments vary in proportion to the difficulty of the tests put to children. Some assert that there is evidence of at least elementary reasoning in children three years old: others claim that the ability of reason does not develop until the seventh year.[29]

The age of discretion for the reception of Holy Communion is the same as the age of discretion for the reception of sacramental absolution.[30] Canonists and theologians have interpreted the phrase *"postquam ad annos discretionis,"* as found in the decree *Omnis utriusque* of the IV General Council of the Lateran, as denoting the age at which a child becomes *doli capax.* The glossator to the Decretals of Pope Gregory IX, wherein the decree *Omnis utriusque* is repeated, understood the attaining of the years of discretion in this sense.[31] Many contemporary writers who followed this interpretation taught that a child became *doli capax,* that is, capable of committing sin

incipit obligatio satisfaciendi utrique praecepto Confessionis et Communionis."—*AAS,* II (1910), 582; *Fontes,* n. 2103.

The canons of the Code do not derogate from the norms of the decree *Quam singulari.* According to canon 6, universal laws are abolished only if they are opposed to the canons of the Code. The decree in question enjoyed the force of universal law, and the norms contained therein, so far from being opposed to the canons of the Code, help towards their better understanding. The only difference lies in the viewpoint of the legislator. The norms of the decree were calculated to extirpate the existing abuse of demanding a too advanced age for the reception of Holy Communion: the law contained in the Code is designed to check the opposite abuse of those who would allow children to approach the altar with little or no preparation.—Cf. Vermeersch-Creusen, *Epitome Iuris Canonici,* II, 70.

[29] Cf. Munn, *op. cit.,* pp. 367-368.

[30] S. C. de Sacramentis, decr. 8 aug. 1910: "Quos reprehendimus abusus ex eo sunt repetendi, quod nec scite nec recte definiverint, quaenam sit aetas discretionis, qui aliam Poenitentiae, aliam Eucharistiae assignarunt. Unam tamen eandemque aetatem ad utrumque Sacramentum requirit Lateranense Concilium, quum coniunctum Confessionis et Communionis onus imponit."—*AAS,* II (1910), 580; *Fontes,* n. 2103.

[31] C. 12, X, *de poenitentiis et remissionibus,* V, 38, ad v. "discretionis:"—". . . id est, cum est doli capax: quia tunc potest peccare . . ."

or of violating the law, at about the age of seven.[32] This capacity to violate the law, whether that law be divine law or human law, postulates both that degree of intellectual development which suffices for an understanding of the law and, in addition, that measure of freedom for acting which allows the act to be regarded as a human act.[33] There are two essential notes, then, in the concept of the use of reason: the presence of an intellectual development and the exercise of a will that is free.

During the post-Trindentine period theologians disputed concerning the age at which a child attained the use of reason. Many of them taught that the age of discretion for the reception of Holy Communion was attained between the tenth and the twelfth year, while others asserted that a child began to enjoy the use of reason at about its seventh year.[34] In more recent times the controversy on the precise meaning of the phrase *doli capax* has centered, not on the number of years which must elapse from birth before a child becomes capable of committing sin, but on whether the capacity to commit sin should be understood as referring exclusively to mortal sin, or also inclusively to venial sin.[35]

An attempt to obtain a decision on this controversy was made by the Bishop of Norcia when he asked the Commission for the Authentic Interpretation of the Code whether the use of reason as postulated in the law had to be such that a child be capable of committing mortal sin, or whether it sufficed that it have the capacity to commit venial sin. The reply of the Commission, given on February 24, 1920, was not as specific and direct an answer as might have been formulated. It stated, in a very general way, that the

[32] Cf. Gillman, "Die *'anni discretionis'* im Kanon *'Omnis utriusque sexus'* "—*Archiv für katholisches Kierchenrecht* (Vols. I-VI, Innsbruck, 1857-1861; Vols. VII—, Mainz, 1862—), CVIII (1928), 556-617, esp. pp. 560, 564, 570 (hereafter the *Archiv* is cited *AKKR*).

[33] Cf. Michiels, *Normae Generales Iuris Canonici* (2 vols., Lublin: Universitas Catholica, 1929), I, 291; Ojetti, *Commentarium in Codicem Iuris Canonici* (4 vols., Romae: Universitas Gregoriana, 1927-1931), I, 103; Berutti, *Institutiones Iuris Canonici* (6 vols., Vol. I, Taurini-Romae: Marietti, 1936), I, 77.

[34] Cf. *supra*, pp. 13 ff.

[35] Cf. Cappello, *De Sacramentis*, I, 389; Coronata, *Tractatus Canonicus de Sacramentis*, I, 291.

requisite use of reason for the reception of Holy Communion was indicated clearly in canon 854, §§ 2-3, and with reference to the precept of annual confession, in canon 906.[86] Since this response did not appear in the official organ of the Holy See, namely the *Acta Apostolicae Sedis,* it cannot be regarded as an officially authentic interpretation which compels universal recognition.

However, the controversy just mentioned has little practical value for the purposes here pursued. The relevant point is this: when a child becomes capable of breaking the law or of committing sin, it has reached the age of discretion. Such indications as the following show that a child has reached the use of reason: acknowledgement of malice in its external acts, confusion and shame after committing some fault, or an externally manifested advertence to the fact that it has done wrong. The fact that a child can recognize its parents or friends is not a certain indication that it is capable of exercising its reasoning powers. Such recognition can be merely sensory, as distinct from intellectual, recognition. Cappello had recommended this latter test in his pre-Code commentary on the decree *Quam singulari.*[87] It is significant that he has omitted mention of this particular test in the recent (1945) edition of his commentary on the sacraments.[88]

The mentioned tests, applicable to all children who have been taught to distinguish between good and evil, will be especially useful for discerning whether children, if they have no knowledge of the Eucharist, actually enjoy the use of reason. As will be shown in the following paragraphs, there are other tests, applicable only to children who have been educated in matters of faith, which will show whether a child enjoys the use of reason, and whether at the same time it possesses the knowledge required by the canons for the reception of Holy Communion.

[86] "Dubium. Utrum usus rationis de quo in cc. 854, §§ 2, 3, 5; 859, § 1, et 906, is intelligatur qui ad mortale peccatum requiritur, an sufficiat qui requiritur ad peccatum veniale committendum?—R. Usus rationis pro sancta Communione indicatur clare in c. 854, §§ 2, 3; pro praecepto confessionis annuae est qui indicatur in c. 906."—*AKKR,* CI (1921), 68.

[87] *De aetate admittendorum ad primam Communionem Eucharisticam.*

[88] *De Sacramentis,* I, 389.

It must be borne in mind that the enjoyment of the use of reason does not in itself warrant the admission of children to the reception of the Holy Eucharist. The general law, stated in canon 859, § 1, which obliges to the reception of Holy Communion all the faithful who have reached the years of discretion, must be taken in conjunction with canon 854, §§ 1-3, if it is to be fully and properly understood.[39]

This latter canon, in the three paragraphs or sections just quoted, demands a certain development both of the intellect and of the will before the Eucharist may lawfully be administered. In other words, the law by which children are bound to receive Holy Communion may be stated thus: children are bound to receive the Eucharist at Paschal time after they have reached the years of discretion, provided that they are qualified to receive Holy Communion in view of their possession of that knowledge and devotion which are specified in canon 854, §§ 2-3. The minimum requirements, as mentioned in paragraph 2 of this canon, are applicable only to children who are in danger of death. Such children must be able to distinguish the Body of Christ from common bread, and be ready to adore It reverently, before they can be admitted to Holy Communion. Outside the danger of death somewhat more perfect dispositions are demanded on the part both of the intellect and of the will. Canon 854, § 3, requires that, when the danger of death does not exist, a child have a knowledge of those mysteries of the faith which are necessary as a means to salvation, the knowledge being proportionate to the child's capacity for understanding, and in addition that the child must approach the altar for Holy Communion with a devotion that corresponds at least to the limited capacity of its tender years.

In practice, then, whenever there is question of deciding the

[39] Canon 854, § 1. Pueris, qui propter aetatis imbecillitatem nondum huius sacramenti cognitionem et gustum habent, Eucharistia ne ministretur.

§ 2—In periculo mortis, ut sanctissima Eucharistia pueris ministrari possit ac debeat, satis est ut sciant Corpus Christi a communi cibo discernere illudque reverenter adorare.

§ 3—Extra mortis periculum plenior cognitio doctrinae christianae et accuratior praeparatio merito exigitur, ea scilicet, quo ipsi fidei saltem mysteria necessaria necessitate medii ad salutem pro suo captu percipiant, et devote pro suae aetatis modulo ad sanctissimam Eucharistiam accedant.

fitness of children for Holy Communion when they have received a Catholic education in matters of faith, the one set of tests will indicate whether they enjoy the use of reason and whether at the same time they possess the knowledge required by law for their admission to Holy Communion. The movement of the will follows the deliberation of the intellect. A child whose intellect is so developed that it can distinguish the Body of Christ from common bread, and understand in some way the truths which are necessary for salvation, and whose acts of the will at the same time correspond to this knowledge through adoration of and reverent devotion to the Holy Eucharist, certainly enjoys the use of reason.

The contention that sufficient indications of the presence of the use of reason are provided by the fact that a child enjoys those dispositions of the intellect and of the will which are mentioned in canon 854 is in full accord with the teaching contained in the decree *Quam singulari.* The relevant section of this decree stated that the age of discretion for the reception of Holy Communion was that age at which a child could distinguish the Eucharist from common corporeal bread and approach the altar with devotion.[40] The private response of the Commission for the Authentic Interpretation of the Code already referred to likewise substantiates that claim.[41] It is true that the response is not officially authentic in character, yet it at least indicates the mind of the Commission on the point.

The writer is by no means attempting to distinguish between the age of discretion for Holy Communion and the age of discretion for confession. Considered abstractly, the age of discretion or the amount of the use of reason which must be had is the same for both.[42] The difference lies solely in the tests or proofs invoked for detecting whether a child enjoys the use of reason. Those tests must be adapted to the type of intellectual knowledge which it is postulated for the child to possess. Since the knowledge required for the reception of sacramental absolution differs from the knowledge required

[40] "Ex quibus omnibus colligitur aetatem discretionis ad Communionem eam esse, in quae puer panem eucharisticum a pane communi et corporali distinguere sciat ut ad altare possit devote accedere."—*AAS,* II (1910), 581; *Fontes,* n. 2103.

[41] Cf. *supra,* p. 45, footnote 36, for the text of this response.

[42] Cf. canons 859, § 1, and 906.

for the reception of Holy Communion, it follows that tests to indicate the presence of this knowledge and the ability to place the corresponding acts of the will must also differ.

Section 3. The Beginning of the Obligation

Theologians and canonists agree that, though the obligation to receive Holy Communion begins to bind children when they have reached the use of reason, they are not bound on that account to receive immediately. The school of authors who distinguish the capacity to commit mortal sin from the capacity to commit venial sin arrives at this conclusion by arguing as follows: The obligation to receive sacramental absolution begins to bind when a child has developed the ability to commit mortal sin. Since the obligation to receive Holy Communion begins at the same time, a child is not bound to approach the altar until it is capable of committing mortal sin. A child which has just attained the use of reason is not yet capable of committing mortal sin, and hence it is not bound to receive the Eucharist immediately.[43]

Those who assert that the ability to commit venial sin connotes also the ability to commit mortal sin contend that children are not obliged to receive Holy Communion immediately after attaining the years of discretion in view of the fact that the precept to communicate is an affirmative precept which requires only that the Eucharist be received once within a specific period.[44]

If there is not excusing cause, the obligation to receive the Eucharist must be fulfilled during the Paschal season which follows the attaining of the years of discretion. This is immediately evident from the words of canon 859, § 1. A reasonable cause must be had if the fulfillment of the obligation is to be permissibly postponed beyond the Paschal period. In general it may be stated that the cause must be such as benefits the spiritual welfare of a child if the

[43] Cf. Coronata, *Tractatus Canonicus de Sacramentis*, I, 311.

[44] "Sane praeceptum, utpote affirmativum, obligat quidem semper, at non pro semper; seu *incipit* quidem obligare ubi primum ad annos discretionis puer pervenerit, sed non ita tamen ut *illico* sit eidem satisfaciendum."—Cappello, *De Sacramentis*, I, 391.

cause is to be considered a reasonable one. Thus it would be quite lawful to postpone the First Holy Communion of a child in order to secure a better preparation or a better education in christian doctrine. The mere wish of parents or other interested parties that Holy Communion be postponed until after the Paschal season would not be a reasonable cause.

The Code does not acknowledge any right for parents or guardians to decide what constitutes a reasonable cause. It designates the one who can exercise this right by employing the term *proprius sacerdos.* This term is interpreted as meaning either the pastor or the confessor.[45] Granted the existence of a reasonable cause, either the pastor or the confessor can postpone the reception of Holy Communion *ad tempus.* The phrase *ad tempus* must not be taken as the equivalent of indefinitely, but rather as meaning until such time as the cause for postponement has ceased.

It is clear from what has been said that the reception of the Eucharist is conditioned on the enjoyment of the use of reason and, in addition, on the prescribed preparation. It has been pointed out that, even though a child *may* receive Holy Communion when it is thus qualified, it is not *obliged* to do so until the advent of the Paschal season. A further question now arises: Is a child which has reached the use of reason and which has been duly prepared, but which has not yet completed its seventh year, bound to receive Holy Communion at Paschal time?

One school of canonists and theologians maintains that the obligation to receive Holy Communion during the Paschal season binds only when a child has completed its seventh year.[46] The protagonists of this doctrine assert that the norm of canon 12, which demands

[45] Vermeersch-Creusen, *Epitome Iuris Canonici,* II, 77; Cappello, *op. cit.*, I, 391; Prümmer, *Manuale Theologiae Moralis,* III, 158; Gasparri, *De Sanctissima Eucharistia.* II, 379, n. 1156; Fanfani, *De Iure Parochorum* (Taurini-Romae: Marietti, 1924), p. 253; Woywod, *A Practical Commentary on the Code of Canon Law* (9. ed., 2 vols., New York: Wagner, 1945), I, 414; Durieux-Dolphin, *The Eucharist, Law and Practice* (Chicago: The Lakeside Press, 1926), p. 172.

[46] E.g., Augustine, *A Commentary on Canon Law* (8 vols., Vol. IV, 3. ed., 1925, St. Louis: Herder), IV, 227; Noldin-Schmitt, *Summa Theologiae Moralis,* III, 143.

the use of reason and the completion of thc seventh year for subjection to purely ecclesiastical laws, must be applied when a decision is to be made whether such children are bound, since canon 859, § 1, contains no express exception to the general law expressed in canon 12.[47]

To appreciate the force of their argument one must remember that the obligation of approaching the altar during the Paschal season contains two elements—the divine-ecclesiastical obligation of annual Communion, and the obligation of the purely ecclesiastical law of communicating during the Paschal period.

It is difficult to see how their view can be defended. The provisions of canon 12 do not apply when other qualifications for subjection to ecclesiastical law are expressly provided by the Code. Canon 859, § 1, delineates as subjects to the obligation of communicating during the Paschal period all the faithful of either sex who have reached the age of discretion. As has been shown, the age of discretion is not determined by the completion of a certain number of years. Obviously, then, canon 859, § 1, contains an exception to the general law of canon 12.

A response of the Commission for the Authentic Interpretation of the Code, given on January 3, 1918, in reply to a query of the Bishop of Valleyfield, proves this. The doubt that was proposed and the response that was given read as follows:

> Utrum pueri, qui etsi septimum aetatis annum nondum expleverunt, tamen ob aetatem discretionis seu usum rationis ad primam Communionem admissi iam fuerint, teneantur duplici praecepto confessionis saltem semel in anno et Communionis semel in anno, saltem in Paschate?
> *Resp.* Affirmative. Et ratio in aperto est. Nam quamvis canon 12 statuat: "legibus mere ecclesiasticis non tenentur . . . qui, licet rationis usum assecuti, septimum aetatis annum nondum expleverunt," subdit tamen; "nisi aliud iure expresse caveatur."

[47] Canon 12. Legibus mere ecclesiasticis non tenentur qui baptismum non receperunt, nec baptizati qui sufficienti rationis usu non gaudent, nec qui, licet rationis usum assecuti, septimum aetatis annum nondum expleverunt, nisi aliud iure expresse caveatur.

Iamvero in can. 859, § 1, et canon 906 expresse cavetur: "omnis utriusque sexus fidelis postquam ad annos discretionis, idest ad usum rationis, pervenerit" etc.[48]

This response treats explicitly only of the obligation of children who have already been admitted to First Holy Communion. But implicitly it supplies an affirmative answer to the question: Are children who have attained the age of discretion, and who are consequently bound by the divine-ecclesiastical precept of receiving Holy Communion annually, bound also by the purely ecclesiastical precept of going to Holy Communion during the Paschal season? The fact that children have already been admitted to Holy Communion has no essential bearing on the obligation to receive the Eucharist at Paschal time. The phrase in the proposed *dubium* which reads, "children . . . who have already been admitted to First Holy Communion because they have reached the age of discretion or the use of reason," is the equivalent of the phrase, "children . . . who enjoy the use of reason, as is shown by the fact that the ecclesiastical authority has admitted them to Holy Communion." [49]

The response of the Commission explicitly states that children who have attained the use of reason and who have been admitted to First Holy Communion, though they have not yet completed their seventh year, are bound to approach the altar again at Paschal time. Implicitly it states that children who have reached the use of reason are bound to go to Holy Communion at Paschal time, even though they have not yet completed their seventh year.[50]

The official authenticity of this response has been questioned on the ground that the response was not promulgated by means of publication in the *Acta Apostolicae Sedis*.[51] However, according to canon 17, § 2, a declaratory interpretation of law does not require

[48] *Ius Pontificium* (Romae, 1921—), I (1921), 5; Sartori, *Enchiridion Canonicum* (6. ed., Vicetiae: Ex Typographia Commerciali, 1938), pp. 19-20; Bouscaren, *The Canon Law Digest* (2 vols., Milwaukee: Bruce Publishing Company, 1934-1943), I, 53-54.

[49] Cf. Cicognani, *Canon Law* (Philadelphia: Dolphin Press, 1934), p. 573.

[50] Cf. Ojetti, *Commentarium in Codicem Iuris Canonici*, I, 103; Michiels, *Normae Generales Iuris Canonici*, I, 294.

[51] Cf. canon 9 regarding the promulgation of laws issued by the Holy See.

a previous publication in order to exert a binding force.[52] A declaratory interpretation denotes the explanation of a law which, though it be objectively clear and certain in itself, has remained subjectively doubtful in meaning. The interpretation serves simply as an even clearer expression of the law.[53] The fact that the above mentioned response of the Commission must be regarded as a declaratory interpretation of the law is clear from the whole tenor of the reply itself. The response states that the reason for an affirmative reply is obvious, since canon 859, § 1, contains an express exception to the general law contained in canon 12.[54]

Section 4. Presumed Use of Reason

> **Can. 88, 3. Impubes, ante plenum septennium, dicitur infans seu puer vel parvulus et censetur non sui compos: expleto autem septennio, usum rationis habere praesumitur. Infanti assimilantur quotquot usu rationis sunt habitu destituti.**

A child is regarded as not having attained the age of discretion until it has completed its seventh year. When the seventh year has been completed it is presumed that a child enjoys the use of reason. The time of the completion of the seventh year is computed according to canon 34, § 3, 3°.[55] The date of birth is not counted as a day, and the seventh year is regarded as completed on the expiration

[52] Can. 17, § 2. Interpretatio authentica, per modum legis exhibita, eandem vim habet ac lex ipsa; et si verba legis in se certa declaret tantum, promulgatione non eget et valet retrorsum.

[53] Cf. Beste, *Introductio in Codicem* (ed. altera, Collegeville: St. John's Abbey Press, 1944), p. 76; Van Hove, *De Legibus Ecclesiasticis* (Mechliniae-Romae: Dessain, 1930), p. 248.

[54] Cf. Blat, *De Sacramentis*, p. 195.

[55] Si terminus *a quo* non coincidat cum initio diei, ex. gr., *decimus quartus aetatis annus, annus novitiatus, octiduum a vacatione sedis episcopalis, decendium ad appellandum*, etc., prima dies ne computetur et tempus finiatur expleto ultimo die eiusdem numeri.

of the same date seven years later. Thus a child born on May 8, 1936, is regarded in law as having completed its seventh year at midnight May 8-May 9, 1943.

In practice however the completion of the seventh year has little to do with the decision of the question whether a child has reached the age of discretion for the reception of first Holy Communion. Canon 88, § 3, establishes simply a presumption of law. Such a presumption yields to contrary proof. The method of disproving a presumption of law depends on the nature of the presumption. A legally acknowledged presumption (*iuris simpliciter*) admits of both direct and indirect proof to the contrary; a legally mandatory presumption (*iuris et de iure*) can be only indirectly impugned.[56]

Direct proof to the contrary is obtained when despite an admission of fact on which the presumption is based one has proved the falsity of the consequences which presumably follow from this concession. Indirect proof to the contrary is obtained when one has successfully impugned the very fact on which the presumption is based. Coronata asserts that the presumption mentioned in canon 88, § 3, is a legally mandatory presumption (*iuris et de iure*), and that consequently it can be only indirectly impugned.[57] But it is the common opinion that the presumption in question is simply a legally acknowledged presumption (*iuris simpliciter*) and that consequently it can be attacked both directly and indirectly.[58]

It is not lawful therefore to conclude that the completion of the seventh year marks the beginning of the age of discretion for the reception of first Holy Communion. One must give attention to the

[56] Canon 1826.

[57] *Institutiones Iuris Canonici ad Usum Utriusque Cleri et Scholarum* (5 vols., Vols., I-IV, 2. ed., 1939-1945, Vol. V, 1936, Taurini: Marietti), I, 135.

[58] Beste, *Introductio in Codicem*, p. 808; Wernz-Vidal, *Ius Canonicum ad Codicis Normam Exactum* (7 tomes in 8 vols., Vol. IV, Pars. 2, 1935, Vol. VI, 1927, Romae: Apud Aedes Universitatis Gregorianae), VI, 466, footnote 9 (hereafter cited *Ius Canonicum*); Cocchi, *Commentarium in Codicem Iuris Canonici* (8 vols. in 5, Vol. VI, 3. ed., 1933, Vol. VII, 3. ed., 1940, Taurinorum Augustae: Marietti), VII, 300 (hereafter cited *Commentarium in Codicem*); Noval, *Commentarium Codicis Iuris Canonici, Lib. IV, De Processibus* (2 vols., Romae, 1920-1932), I, 376.

mental development of each individual child in determining when it begins to enjoy the use of reason. It has been pointed out that the time of the beginning of the use of reason varies in individual cases. A pastor would therefore be acting unlawfully if he demanded the completion of the seventh year in every case before allowing children to make their first Communion.

CHAPTER IV

DISPOSITIONS REQUIRED FOR FIRST HOLY COMMUNION

THE Council of Trent taught that one could receive the sacrament of the Eucharist in three possible ways according as one furnished variable dispositions in the approach to its reception: It could be received:

(1) Sacramentally, that is, as when received unfruitfully by a sinner;

(2) Spiritually, that is, when the faithful, motivated by faith and charity, receive the fruits of the sacrament by reception of desire;

(3) Sacramentally and spiritually, that is, when Holy Communion is received worthily and fruitfully.[1]

Theologians expanded and explained this threefold division of the Council of Trent. They distinguished the real reception of Holy Communion, that is, the actual reception of the Consecrated Host, from the purely spiritual reception. The real reception was a merely material one on the part of those who were incapable of receiving Holy Communion as a sacrament; it was a sacramental reception, on the part of those who were capable of receiving the Eucharist as a sacrament.

[1] Sess. XIII, *de Eucharistia*, c. 8: "Quoad usum autem, recte et sapienter patres nostri tres rationes hoc sanctum sacramentum accipiendi distinxerunt. Quosdam enim docuerunt sacramentaliter dumtaxat id sumere, ut peccatores; alios tantum spiritualiter, illos nimirum, qui voto propositum illum coelestem panem edentes, fide viva, quae per dilectionem operatur, fructum eius et utilitatem sentiunt; tertios porro sacramentaliter simul et spiritualiter; hi autem sunt, qui ita se prius probant et instruunt, ut vestem nuptialem induti, ad divinam hanc mensam accedant. . . ." Schroeder, *Canons and Decrees of the Council of Trent*, pp. 354-355.

Article 1. Spiritual Dispositions

Section 1. Disposition of the Soul: the State of Grace

Since the Eucharist is a sacrament of the living, it presupposes the state of grace in him who receives it. Should a baptized person approach the altar in the state of mortal sin, he would indeed really receive the Eucharist, but only sacramentally, that is, without any spiritual profit. Freedom from mortal sin is a necessary prerequisite for the fruitful reception of Holy Communion.[2]

Venial sin, while impeding to some extent the gaining of the greater benefits which can be derived from a more worthy reception of the Eucharist, does not destroy the efficacy of the sacrament. A person guilty of venial sin has the right to seek sacramental absolution for the purpose of disposing himself more perfectly for the worthier reception of Holy Communion.

After reaching the years of discretion all the faithful of both sexes are bound by the ecclesiastical precept of annual confession.[3] In order to understand this precept correctly it is necessary to bear in mind the fact that the obligation to seek sacramental absolution binds only those who have committed a mortal sin which has not yet been directly remitted.[4] Hence, strictly taken, the subjects of the

[2] Conc. Trident. sess. XIII, *de Eucharistia,* c. 7: "Si non decet ad sacras ullas functiones quempiam accedere nisi sancte, certe quo magis sanctitas et divinitas coelestis huius sacramenti viro christiano comperta est, eo diligentius cavere ille debet, ne absque magna reverentia et sanctitate ad id percipiendum accedat, praesertim cum illa plena formidinis verba apud Apostolum legamus: '*Qui manducat et bibit indigne, iudicium sibi manducat et bibit, non diiudicans corpus Domini.*' "—Schroeder, *Canons and Decrees of the Council of Trent,* p. 354.

[3] Canon 906. Omnis utriusque sexus fidelis, postquam ad annos discretionis, idest ad usum rationis pervenerit, tenetur omnia peccata sua saltem semel in anno fideliter confiteri.

[4] Canon 901. Qui post baptismum mortalia perpetravit, quae nondum per claves Ecclesiae directe remissa sunt, debet omnia quorum post diligentem sui discussionem conscientiam habeat, confiteri et circumstantias in confessione explicare, quae speciem peccati mutent.

precept of annual confession are those who have attained the use of reason and who are conscious of mortal sin.[5]

Children who have reached the use of reason are capable subjects of the precept of annual confession. Even if their conscience is not burdened with mortal sin, they still have the right to seek sacramental absolution for the venial sins which they may have committed. The decree *Quam singulari* defined the age for confession as that age at which children can distinguish right from wrong.[6] At this age children are capable of receiving sacramental absolution, and confessors are bound in justice to absolve them if they find them properly disposed. The custom of not allowing children to make a sacramental confession before receiving first Holy Communion has been reprobated by the Holy See.[7]

It may easily happen that children have but doubtfully sufficient matter to confess. The rules given by St. Alphonsus Liguori (1696-1787) offer a practical solution for the problem whether absolution should or should not be imparted. If children confess a doubtful matter which is related to mortal sin, they should be conditionally absolved, lest perchance they remain without sanctifying grace. If the doubtfully sufficient matter confessed by them relates to venial sin, they should likewise be conditionally absolved in two cases, name-

[5] Cf. Coronata, *Tractatus Canonicus de Sacramentis,* I, 499; Prümmer, *Manuale Theologiae Moralis,* III, 258; Noldin-Schmitt, *Summa Theologiae Moralis,* II, 641; Vermeersch-Creusen, *Epitome Iuris Canonici,* II, 109; Regatillo, *Ius Sacramentarium* (2 vols., Santander: Sal Terrae, 1945-1946), I, 212; Vermeersch, *Theologia Moralis* (2 ed., 4 vols., Romae: Universita Gregoriana, 1926-1928), III, 482.

[6] "Igitur, quemadmodum ad Confessionem aetas discretionis ea censetur, in qua honestum ab inhonesto distingui potest, nempe quo ad usum rationis pervenitur: . . ."—*AAS,* II (1910), 580; *Fontes,* n. 2103.

[7] S. C. de Sacramentis, decr. 8 aug. 1910: "Nec minus est reprobandus mos pluribus vigens locis quo sacramentalis Confessio inhibetur pueris nondum ad eucharisticam mensam admissis, aut iisdem absolutio non impertitur. Quo fit ut ipsi peccatorum fortasse gravium laqueis irretiti magno cum periculo diu iaceant."—*AAS,* II (1910), 579; *Fontes,* n. 2103. N. VII: "Consuetudo non admittendi ad confessionem pueros, aut numquam eos absolvendi, quum ad usum rationis pervenerint, est omnino improbanda. Quare Ordinarii locorum, adhibitis etiam remediis iuris, curabunt ut penitus de medio tollatur."—*AAS,* II (1910), 583; *Fontes,* n. 2103.

ly, when there is question of fulfilling the paschal precept, or when there is danger of death.[8] The confession of imperfections does not in itself warrant the giving of sacramental absolution. However, prudent questioning on the part of the confessor will often reveal the existence of venial faults at the root of these imperfections.[9]

The problem concerning the necessity of confession for newly baptized adults may now be considered. Canon 753, § 2, recommends that adult neophytes assist at Mass and receive Holy Communion immediately after the ceremony of baptism, unless grave and urgent reasons prevent this.[10] Are such persons bound to confess before they receive their first Holy Communion?

To answer this question properly it is necessary to distinguish between the absolute baptism conferred on converts from paganism and the conditional baptism given to converts from heretical sects. Sins committed before baptism are remitted by the sacrament of baptism validly and fruitfully received. They are remitted at the time of baptism if that sacrament was received with attrition for past sins. If the baptism was received without such attrition on the part of the recipient, then his sins are remitted later when he supplies the lacking act of attrition. Hence neophytes from paganism are not bound to confess their pre-baptismal sins before the reception of their first Holy Communion.

The problem of the necessity of confession on the part of persons who have been conditionally baptized is somewhat more complicated. If the conditionally baptized party has already made a worthy confession after his first baptism, then another confession of these same sins after his reception of conditional baptism is not required. If the first baptism was valid, then the sacramental absolution already received was valid; if the first baptism was invalid, then of course the imparted sacramental absolution was also without effect, but both the original sin and also the personal sins were then remitted through the conditionally conferred baptism, which in the given assumption was in fact an absolute baptism.

[8] *Theologia Moralis,* Lib. VI, *de Poenitentia,* n. 432.

[9] Cf. Vermeersch, *Theologia Moralis,* I, 172.

[10] Nisi graves urgentesque causae obsint, adultus baptizatus statim Missae sacrificio assistat et sacram communionem percipiat.

Theologians disagree on the point whether an obligation of confessing exists when a person who has never made a worthy confession after his first baptism later received baptism conditionally. Some deny the existence of any such obligation,[11] while others assert that in such circumstances a neophyte is bound to make a sacramental confession for the purpose of receiving a conditional absolution from his confessed sins.[12] The latter opinion seems the more acceptable one in view of the fact that the Holy Office has on various occasions recommended confession with conditional absolution for conditionally baptized converts. In the United States,[13] England,[14] the Philippine Islands, [15] and in the archdiocese of Dublin, Ireland,[16] priests are required to hear the confessions of the conditionally baptized neophyte and to grant him conditional absolution from the sins he has confessed.

Section 2. Dispositions of the Will

A. Intention

Intention is defined as an act of the will by which that faculty efficaciously desires to reach an end by employing the necessary means.[17] Since the knowledge of the intellect paves the way for the deliberation of the will, it follows that the intention to receive Holy Communion is the desire to communicate in order to profit by the treasures which the Eucharist is known to contain.

For the valid reception of the sacraments, with the exception of the Eucharist, a true intention of receiving them is required in

[11] E. g., Cappello, *De Sacramentis,* I, 135; Coronata, *Tractatus Canonicus de Sacramentis,* I, 436; Regatillo, *Ius Sacramentarium,* I, 217.

[12] E. g., Prümmer, *Manuale Theologiae Moralis,* III, 106; O'Kane-Fallon, *Notes on the Rubrics of the Roman Ritual* (4. ed., Dublin: Duffy, 1938), pp. 217-218.

[13] S. C. S. Off., decr. 20 iul. 1859—*Collect.,* n. 1178; *Fontes,* n. 953. Cf. *The Priest's New Ritual* (Baltimore: Murphy, 1940), p. 49.

[14] S. C. S. Off., decr. 17 dec. 1868—*Collect.,* n. 1338; cf. also S. C. S. Off., decr. 27 iun. 1715—*Collect.,* 286; *Fontes,* n. 780.

[15] Cf. Regatillo, *Ius Sacramentarium,* I, 217.

[16] Cf. O'Kane-Fallon, *op. cit.,* p. 217, footnote 3.

[17] Pohle-Preuss, *The Sacraments,* I, 175.

adults. In the present dispensation God does not will to sanctify men without their consent. The word "adults" is here understood to have the meaning which the Code attaches to it when it deals with the subject of baptism, that is, as pointing to those persons who enjoy the use of reason.[18] The Eucharist, however, can be truly received independently of any intention on the part either of the minister or of the recipient, for it consists of something permanent. An intention on the part of the recipient is necessary however for the fruitful reception of this sacrament.[19]

Theologians and canonists agree that a habitual intention, explicit outside the danger of death, implicit in danger of death, is indeed required, but also suffices, for the fruitful reception of Holy Communion.[20] A habitual intention is one which, though once elicited and never revoked, nevertheless does not actually influence the act when it is placed.[21] Regarding the reception of Holy Communion such a habitual intention is designated as explicit if the previously elicited act of the will actually centered upon the reception of the sacraments; it is called implicit if the elicited act of the will simply tended to the exercise of a conduct in accord with the teachings and the commandments of Christ and the Church. Since a habitual intention suffices for the fruitful reception of the Eucharist, it follows, *a fortiori,* that an actual or a virtual intention suffices.

The intention of receiving Holy Communion must be true and sincere. The communicant must will to receive the Eucharist for the sake of gaining an increase of sanctifying grace, and not, for example, for the sake of imitating others who receive, or of pleasing

[18] Canon 745, § 2, 2°. Adulti autem censentur, qui rationis usu fruuntur; . . .

[19] Tanquerey, *Synopsis Theologiae Dogmaticae,* III, 307-308.

[20] Cappello, *De Sacramentis,* I, 401; Noldin-Schmitt, *Summa Theologiae Moralis,* III, 135; Durieux-Dolphin, *The Eucharist, Law and Practice,* p. 176; Davis, *Moral and Pastoral Theology* (4. ed., 4 vols., New York: Sheed and Ward, 1943), III, 207; Telch, *Epitome Theologiae Moralis* (6. ed., Oeniponte: Rauch, 1924), p. 254; De Smet, *Tractatus Dogmatico-Moralis de Sacramentis in Genere* (ed. altera, Brugis: Beyaert, 1924), pp. 134-135; Regatillo, *Ius Sacramentarium,* I, 23.

[21] Cf. Pohle- Preuss, *op. cit.,* I, 176; Noldin-Schmitt, *Summa Theologiae Moralis,* I, 53.

his parents. An explanation of what constitutes a right intention in this regard was furnished by Pope Pius X (1903-1914) in the decree *Sacra Tridentina Synodus.* This decree dealt explicitly with frequent Communion, but the relevant norm contained therein was equally applicable to the intention requisite for the fruitful reception of first Holy Communion. According to Pope Pius, a right intention consists in this that the communicant acts not through vanity or from human considerations, but with the desire of satisfying the will of God, of uniting himself to God more intimately through charity, and of making use of the divinely prescribed remedy for his infirmities and failings.[22]

It is to be recommended that children be taught to propose these motives to themselves when they are about to approach the altar for the first time. Nevertheless it is not necessary that they be thus motivated explicitly. It suffices for the fruitful reception of Holy Communion if the stated motives be included in the general intention of receiving the Eucharist with the desire to profit by the spiritual treasures which it contains.

B. Devotion

It is unbecoming to approach the altar for the reception of the Holy Eucharist except in a spirit of piety and reverence. Holy Communion should be received with sentiments of sincere devotion. All worldly thoughts should be put away and the mind raised to God through fervent acts of faith, hope and charity. It is a venial sin to receive the Eucharist while entertaining wilful distractions.

There is no law by which the faithful are obliged to receive Holy Communion with any definite measure of devotion. Theologians agree that a lack of devotion does not exceed a venial sin, and that the presence of actual devotion is but required for the more fruitful reception of the Eucharist.[23]

[22] "Recta autem mens in eo est, ut qui ad sacram Mensam accedit, non usui aut vanitati aut humanis rationibus indulgeat, sed Dei placito satisfacere velit, ei arctius caritate coniungi, ac divino illo pharmaco suis infirmitatibus ac defectibus occurrere."—*Fontes,* n. 4326.

[23] Pohle-Preuss, *The Sacraments* (3 ed., 4 vols., St. Louis: Herder, 1919-1920), II, 270; Prümmer, *Manuale Theologiae Moralis,* III, 146; Lehmkuhl,

The greater the amount of knowledge about the Blessed Eucharist, the more intense the acts of devotion which can be elicited. The Council of Trent, speaking of the reverence due to the Blessed Sacrament, stated that the more the holiness and divinity of this heavenly sacrament were understood, the greater the reverence with which it should be received.[24] Since children are expected to know and understand the rudiments of doctrine concerning the Eucharist, they cannot be required to possess that degree of devotion which is possible to those of more mature intellect. The Code uses the phrase *"et devote pro suae aetatis modulo"* to indicate that a devotion which is proportioned to the tender years of children is sufficient for their admission to first Holy Communion.[25]

Section 3. Dispositions of the Intellect: Knowledge and Appreciation

Can. 854, § 2. In periculo mortis, ut sanctissima Eucharistia pueris ministrari possit ac debeat, satis est ut sciant Corpus Christi a communi cibo discernere illudque reverenter adorare.

§ 3. Extra mortis periculum plenior cognitio doctrinae christianae et accuratior praeparatio merito exigitur, ea scilicet, qua ipsi fidei saltem mysteria necessaria necessitate medii ad salutem pro suo captu percipiant, et devote pro suae aetatis modulo ad sanctissimam Eucharistiam accedant.

A. Knowledge

A certain amount of intellectual knowledge is required in adults for the fruitful reception of Holy Communion. As has been noted, at least a habitual intention is necessary in adults if they are to receive the Eucharist with profit. Since the acts of the will depend

Theologia Moralis (4. ed., 2 vols., Friburgi-Brisgoviae: Herder, 1887), II, 108-109; Aertnys-Damen, *Theologia Moralis* (13. ed., 2 vols., Taurini-Romae: Marietti, 1939), II, 109.

[24] Sess. XIII, *de Eucharistia,* c. 7—Schroeder, *Canons and Decrees of the Council of Trent,* p. 77.

[25] Canon 854, § 3.

on the deliberations of the intellect, an intention of receiving Holy Communion as a sacrament cannot be formed without some knowledge of what the Eucharist is.

The decree *Quam singulari* did not distinguish between the knowledge required for simple Holy Communion and the knowledge required for Viaticum. It merely directed that children should be able to distinguish the Eucharist from common bread and have a knowledge of the truths necessary in the nature of essential means for salvation.[26] The Code requires a lesser intellectual preparation for the reception of Holy Communion as Viaticum than for the reception of simple Holy Communion.

In danger of death a child is required to be able to distinguish the Body of Christ from common bread. It must be able to understand at least the essential notion of the presence of Christ under the appearances of bread. Such a knowledge connotes a knowledge of the mystery of the Incarnation, since some understanding of this mystery is a necessary preamble to the mystery of the Holy Eucharist. However, as will be pointed out towards the end of this section, no very deep knowledge of either of these mysteries is required for admission to the reception of Viaticum.

Outside the danger of death a fuller knowledge of Christian doctrine is required. Canon 854, § 3, demands that in ordinary circumstances a child must have some knowledge of the mysteries of faith which are necessary as essential means for salvation. The wording of this section of canon 854 shows that this knowledge of the mysteries of faith is required in addition to the basic knowledge of the presence of Christ in the Eucharist.[27]

Explicit belief in the existence of God as the rewarder of the good is an essential condition for the gaining of salvation. Practically all theologians teach this, finding a basis for their assertion in the

[26] N. III: "Cognitio religionis quae in puero requiritur, ut ipse ad primam Communionem convenienter se praeparet, ea est, qua ipse fidei mysteria necessaria necessitate medii pro suo captu percipiat, atque eucharisticum panem a communi et corporali distinguat, ut ea devotione quam ipsius fert aetas ad SS. Eucharistiam accedat."—*AAS*, II (1910), 582; *Fontes*, n. 2103.

[27] Canon 854, § 3." . . . *plenior* cognitio doctrinae . . ." (Italics inserted by the writer).

words of St. Paul: "For he who comes to God must believe that God exists and is rewarder of those who seek him,"[28] and in the condemnation by Pope Innocent XI (1676-1689) of a proposition which stated that faith in one God, but not the explicit faith in God as a rewarder, was necessary as an essential means to salvation.[29]

Theologians are not in agreement on whether an explicit faith in Christ the Redeemer and in the Blessed Trinity is absolutely necessary for salvation. Faith is explicit when assent is given to some truth which is formally known in itself.[30] Those who follow the teaching of St. Thomas (1225-1274) assert that an explicit belief in these two articles of faith is necessary as a means for salvation. The followers of Suarez (1548-1617), on the other hand, absolutely deny this and teach that an implicit faith suffices.[31]

The writer cannot hope to discuss the merits and demerits of the arguments advanced by either side in this theological dispute. In practice, an explicit knowledge of Christ the Redeemer and of the Blessed Trinity should be demanded from children who are about to make their first Holy Communion. A reply of the Holy Office, given on January 25, 1703, stated that missionaries were bound to explain the mysteries which are necessary as essential means, such particularly as the mysteries of the Trinity and of the Incarnation, to dying persons who were not absolutely incapable of receiving such instruction.[32]

Since there is question here of children who are not even in danger of death, it seems very probable that an explicit faith in

[28] Hebrews, XI: 6.

[29] Prop. 22: "Nonnisi fides unius Dei necessaria videtur necessitate medii, non autem explicita Remuneratoris."—Denzinger, n. 1172.

[30] Tanquerey, *Synopsis Theologiae Dogmaticae,* II, 83.

[31] Cf. Prümmer, *Manuale Theologiae Moralis,* I, 350; Cappello, *De Sacramentis,* I, 370; Fanfani, *De Iure Parochorum,* p. 257; Ayrinhac, *Legislation on the Sacraments* (New York: Longmans, Green and Co., 1928), p. 164.

[32] Ad 2: "Non sufficere promissionem, sed missionarium teneri adulto etiam moribundo, qui incapax omnino non sit, explicare mysteria fidei quae sunt necessaria necessitate medii, ut sunt praecipue mysteria Trinitatis et Incarnationis."—*Fontes,* n. 764; *Collect.,* n. 254. This reply was confirmed by Pope Benedict XIV in n. 41 of the Epistle *Postremo mense* of February 28, 1747—*Fontes,* n. 377; *Opera Omnia* (17 vols., Vol. XIV Prati: Ghettus et Soc., 1846), XIV, 183.

the Trinity and in the Incarnation is demanded as an essential means of salvation. In any case, as has already been pointed out, children must know something of the mystery of the Incarnation. The most practical solution for the problem is that given by Tanquerey (1854-1932), who concludes that, since there is question of something necessary for salvation, the safer course should be followed, and consequently all those who have the care of souls should instruct their charges in the mysteries of the Trinity, of the Incarnation, and of the Redemption.[33]

A perfect knowledge of these matters of faith is not demanded as a prerequisite for admission to first Holy Communion.[34] The Code indicates the degree of requisite knowledge by means of the phrase "*pro suo captu.*" In other words, the knowledge that is required must correspond proportionately to the intellectual capacity of a child which has just reached the use of reason. No very deep or scientific knowledge can be expected of children whose mental powers are still comparatively undeveloped. Hence, if a child in its own simple manner knows that God exists, that He will reward the good, that there are three Persons in One God, that Christ, the Second Person of the Blessed Trinity, became Man to redeem the world, and that He is really present in the Eucharist, its intellectual equipment is sufficient for warranting its admission to first Holy Communion.

It does not suffice if children can merely repeat by rote the formulas of doctrine found in approved catechisms. The word "*percipere*," as found in canon 854, § 3, literally means "to lay hold of," and with relation to mental processes means "to comprehend." A child is required to digest and understand in a simple manner the articles of faith mentioned above. The possession of mere vague notions of the necessary doctrines is not a sufficient intellectual preparation for admission to first Holy Communion.[35]

[33] *Synopsis Theologiae Moralis et Pastoralis* (7 ed., 3 vols., Romae: Desclée, 1920), II, 369.

[34] S. C. de Sacramentis, decr. 8 aug. 1910: "Itaque non perfecta rerum Fidei cognitio requiritur, quum aliqua dumtaxat elementa sint satis, hoc est aliqua cognitio; . . ."—*AAS*, II (1910), 581; *Fontes*, n. 2103.

[35] Cf. Schulze, *A Manual of Pastoral Theology* (3. ed., London: Herder, 1939), p. 82. (Reprint of 3. ed., 1923.)

B. Intellectual Appreciation

It is difficult to determine the precise force of the word *"gustus,"* as found in canon 854, § 1. Literally it means "taste" or "relish." Its use by the legislator to indicate some qualification necessary for the reception of Holy Communion is readily understandable in view of the analogy between corporeal and spiritual food. The word was first used in the Catechism of the Council of Trent to denote some qualification in the recipient of the Eucharist.[36]

Gustus is frequently interpreted as meaning "desire" (*desiderium*) or "hunger" (*fames*) or both.[37] This interpretation cannot be justified. In the first place the translation of the word *"gustus"* as meaning "desire" or "hunger" is arbitrary. If the legislator wished to convey the idea of desire or hunger for the Blessed Eucharist it is reasonable to suppose that he would have used the appropriate words, and not a word with an entirely different meaning. In the second place, Gasparri and Coronata, the only two of the authors cited above who attempt to defend their interpretation of the word, fail to substantiate their assertion. They insist that, just as undesired corporeal food does not nourish the body, so neither does undesired spiritual food nourish the soul. It has already been pointed out that the intention of receiving Holy Communion is the desire to receive It in order to profit by the treasures which it contains.[38] Since a habitual intention of receiving, that is, an intention which exercises no actual influence on the act when it is placed, suffices for the fruitful reception of Holy Communion, it follows that the Eucharist can be fruitfully received *even though the desire of communicating exercises no influence on the act.* Hence it is apparent that the explanation of *gustus* as meaning "hunger" or "desire" is not satisfactory.

Cappello's explanation of the word is, in the writer's opinion, the correct one. It has the merit of applying the literal meaning of

[36] ". . . ad illos enim pertinet explorare, et a pueris percunctari, an huius admirabilis sacramenti cognitionem aliquam acceperint, et gustum habeant."—Pars II, *de Eucharistiae Sacramento,* n. 63.

[37] Cf. Gasparri, *De Sanctissima Eucharistia,* II, p. 365, n. 1133; Regatillo, *Ius Sacramentarium,* I, 177; Coronata, *Tractatus Canonicus de Sacramentis,* I, 288; Vermeersch-Creusen, *Epitome Iuris Canonici,* II, 71.

[38] Cf. *supra,* footnote 37.

the word to the qualifications necessary in the recipient of Holy Communion. He explains *"gustus"* as being an act of the intellect rather than an act of the will.[39] *Gustus* is an intellectual relish of, or taste for, the Eucharist. It is an intelligent appreciation which prompts a child to show towards the Sacrament of the Altar a due measure of desire, of reverence, of devotion and of affection[40]

Article 2. Bodily Dispositions

Section 1. The Eucharistic Fast

Can. 858, § 1. Qui a media nocte ieiunium naturale non servaverit, nequit ad sanctissimam Eucharistiam admitti, nisi mortis urgeat periculum, aut necessitas impediendi irreverentiam in sacramentum.

§ 2. Infirmi tamen qui iam a mense decumbunt sine certa spe ut cito convalescant, de prudenti confessarii consilio sanctissimam Eucharistiam sumere possunt semel aut bis in hebdomada, etsi aliquam medicinam vel aliquid per modum potus antea sumpserint.

Authors agree that the law which requires the observance of the natural or the Eucharistic fast before the reception of Holy Communion is a purely ecclesiastical law.[41] Moreover, the completion of

[39] "Cum vero intentio sit actus voluntatis, supponens actum intellectus, sequitur ad sacram communionem cum fructu recipiendam, requiri in adultis cognitionem et gustum huius sacramenti."—*De Sacramentis,* I, 401..

[40] "Gustus autem intelligitur *spiritualis,* non autem sensibilis, quatenus puer erga Eucharistiam ostendat desiderium, reverentiam, pietatem atque affectum."—Cappello, *op. cit.,* I, 370.

[41] Cicognani, *Canon Law,* p. 571; Prümmer, *Manuale Theologiae Moralis,* I, 127; Coronata, *Tractatus Canonicus de Sacramentis,* I, 298; Cappello, *De Sacramentis,* I, 414; Vermeersch-Creusen, *Epitome Iuris Canonici,* II, 73; McCloskey, *The Subject of Ecclesiastical Law according to Canon* 12, The Catholic University of America Canon Law Studies, no. 165 (Washington, D. C.: The Catholic University of America Press, 1942), p. 209; Anglin, *The Eucharistic Fast,* The Catholic University of America Canon Law Studies, no. 124 (Washington, D. C.: The Catholic University of America Press, 1941), p. 117; "Questions des Sciences Ecclésiastiques"—*L'Ami du Clergé* (Paris, 1879—), XLVI (1929), 88-89.

the seventh year is necessary before one becomes subject to purely ecclesiastical laws, unless an express indication to the contrary be given.[42] Canon 858 contains no express exception to the general law as stated in canon 12. Hence, from a strictly canonical viewpoint, children who are admitted to the reception of Holy Communion before they have completed their seventh year are not bound to observe the Eucharistic fast.

Moral theologians, however, argue that such children should be fasting when they receive Holy Communion. They assert that it is best that children be taught to observe this law from the time they begin to communicate, lest in later years they develop false notions as to its gravity. Again, the non-observance of fasting on the part of children not yet seven years of age could readily become a source of scandal to others who do not understand that the law of the Eucharistic fast does not begin to bind until children have completed their seventh year.[43] Hence, in practice, it is better to teach children who have not completed their seventh year to receive Holy Communion only upon the observance of the law of fasting.

It is allowable for one, in order to avoid public scandal, to communicate after one has broken the natural fast.[44] The danger of scandal would be very slight if a child failed to receive the Eucharist on any particular morning. Friends or relatives would easily understand why a child failed to receive if they were told that it had broken its fast. A non-fasting child could not approach the altar merely to avoid disappointment for itself or for its relatives.

One can easily visualize the probability of scandal in the case wherein an adult convert would fail to receive his first Holy Communion on a particular morning. It may well happen that the fact of conversion of a prominent person has become publicly known, and in consequence has become a matter of public interest. In such a case scandal could easily result if such a person failed to receive on the day appointed. Consequently, it would be allowable for such

[42] Canon 12.

[43] Cf. Cicognani, *Canon Law*, p. 571; Anglin, *The Eucharistic Fast*, p. 116.

[44] Prümmer, *Manuale Theologiae Moralis*, III, 152; Regatillo, *Ius Sacramentarium*, I, 74; Cappello, *De Sacramentis*, I, 441.

a convert to approach the altar even though he had broken the Eucharistic fast. An adult neophyte who, in fulfillment of the recommendation of canon 753, § 2, receives Holy Communion immediately after being baptized must in point of fact receive after breaking the Eucharistic fast. The *Roman Ritual* presupposes the swallowing of a pinch of salt as part of the ceremony of baptism.[45]

Canon 858, § 2, explicitly exempts from the observance of the Eucharistic fast those who receive Holy Communion in danger of death and, under certain conditions, those also who have been confined to bed for a month and have no hope of a speedy recovery.[46] Hence, if first Holy Communion is received by way of Viaticum, the fast need not be observed. In hospitals especially there will be cases in which the recipient of first Holy Communion can take medicine or some food by way of drink in view of the fact that he has been confined to bed for a month and there exists as yet no hope of a speedy recovery.

Section 2. External Appearance

Reverence for the Blessed Sacrament demands that Holy Communion be received only when the hands and the face have been properly cleaned. However, dirt and removable stains on these members of the body do not of themselves constitute factors which absolutely stand in the way of the reception of the Eucharist. But circumstances attending such uncleanliness may imply the presence of a venial sin, insofar namely as the tolerated state of uncleanliness denotes a lack of proper respect for this Sacrament, or insofar as it may give rise to an uneasy wonderment among the onlookers.[47]

Consideration must be given to the conditions under which Holy Communion is received if one is to determine whether the approach

[45] Tit. II, c. 4, *Ordo Baptismi Adultorum,* n. 15: "Tunc pollice et indice accipit de ipso sale, et immittit in os Catechumeni, . . ."

[46] For a detailed discussion of the conditions under which Holy Communion can be given to non-fasting sick persons cf. Anglin, *The Eucharistic Fast,* pp. 118-140.

[47] Cf. Vermeersch, *Theologia Moralis,* III, 340; Merkelbach, *Summa Theologiae Moralis,* III, 227; Aertnys-Damen, *Theologia Moralis,* II, 111.

to the altar-rail with dirty hands or face implies the commission of a venial sin. One can readily visualize the case of a soldier convert who, while covered with grime, approaches for his first Holy Communion on a battlefield, but thereby shows no disrespect for the Sacrament and causes no wonderment among the onlookers. In ordinary circumstances however the faithful would be shocked and even scandalized at seeing an unwashed and dirty person approach the altar-rail.

The Code requires that men are to assist at sacred functions with bared head, and that women appear in modest dress and with some head-covering when they receive Holy Communion.[48] In China it is still customary for women to communicate with uncovered head,[49] despite an instruction of the Sacred Congregation for the Propagation of the Faith, given on October 18, 1883, which stated that the Congregation deemed it opportune that there be introduced the custom of requiring women to have their heads covered when they receive the sacrament of Penance or approach the Holy Table.[50] Men or women who violate the requirements of canon 1262, § 2, are not guilty of serious sin if no scandal is occasioned by their action. A reasonable cause suffices to excuse them even from venial sin.[51] Such a cause on the part of men would be the necessity of protecting health.[52]

Women more easily than men can offend against the virtue of modesty in the matter of dress, especially by wearing dresses which are made of flimsy material, which unduly stress the feminine form, or which are cut rather low on the breast. St. Alphonsus disallowed the approach to Holy Communion on the part of women whose bosom was not modestly covered.[53] In an instruction addressed to

[48] Canon 1262, § 2. Viri in ecclesia vel extra ecclesiam, dum sacris ritibus assistunt, nudo capite sint, nisi aliud ferant probati populorum mores aut popularia rerum adiuncta; mulieres autem, capite cooperto et modeste vestitae, maxime cum ad mensam Dominicam accedunt.

[49] Vermeersch-Creusen, *Epitome Iuris Canonici*, II, 362.

[50] XV—*Fontes*, n. 4903; *Collect.*, n. 1606.

[51] Gasparri, *De Sanctissima Eucharistia*, p. 363, n. 1132.

[52] Vermeersch-Creusen, *op. cit.*, II, *loc. cit.*

[53] *Theologia Moralis*, lib. VI, *de Eucharistia*, n. 275.

diocesan ordinaries, and dated January 12, 1930, the Sacred Congregation of the Council stated that girls and women who were immodestly dressed should be refused Holy Communion, and in some cases even excluded from church.[54]

It seems impossible to determine standards of modesty in dress which may be considered as everywhere applicable. Dress which would not give rise to adverse comment or to any occasion for scandal in one district or country might elsewhere be regarded as highly indecorous and irreverent. The custom of individual places and the susceptibility of the people to scandal must always be taken into consideration if one is equitably to determine what constitutes proper dress for the reception of Holy Communion.

Humility in dress as well as modesty is required of communicants. The *Roman Ritual* requires pastors to speak frequently to their people on the necessity of humble dress.[55] Anything which savors of vanity in dress is incompatible with the reception of Him Who is "meek and humble of heart." St. Charles Borromeo (1538-1584) refused to admit to Holy Communion women who wore an elaborate attire, or who had their hair waved or marcelled.[56]

At the present time it could be highly improper to turn away a woman for the simple reason that she had her hair marcelled. Having the hair marcelled is no longer regarded as a sign of vanity. The writer is of the opinion that the word "humble" as used by the *Roman Ritual* should be understood as implying a "quiet" or "subdued" dress as opposed to a gaudy or a flashy apparel. Clothes may be very expensive because of quality or cut, and yet appear quite in harmony with the external reverence with which Holy Communion should be received. It would seem unreasonable to oblige people who are in the habit of wearing expensive clothing to buy a

[54] N. IX: "Puellae et mulieres, quae inhonestas vestes induunt, a Sancta Communione . . . arceantur, atque, si casus ferat, ab ipso ecclesiae ingressu prohibeantur."—*AAS*, XXII (1930), 27; Bouscaren, *Canon Law Digest*, I, 214.

[55] Tit. IV, c. 1, *de sanctissimo Eucharistiae Sacramento*, n. 3: "Ideo populum saepius admonebit, qua praeparatione, et quanta animi religione ac pietate, et humili etiam corporis habitu ad tam divinum Sacramentum debeat accedere: . . ."

[56] *Pastorum Instructiones* (Gandae: Van der Schelden, 1828), pp. 250-251.

cheap and drab attire for use on such occasions. Elegance in dress is not incompatible with Christian modesty and simplicity, nor does the costliness of the material imply a refinement which militates against the called for restraint and unobtrusive mien. If the bearing of the person remains modest and unassuming, then the refinement in dress will prove no hindrance to the requisite bodily dispositions of wholesome reverence and awe.

CHAPTER V

RIGHTS AND DUTIES OF PARENTS, CONFESSORS AND PASTORS

ARTICLE 1. THE DUTY OF PREPARING CHILDREN

Can. 1113. Parentes gravissima obligatione tenentur prolis educationem tum religiosam et moralem, tum physicam et civilem pro viribus curandi, et etiam temporali eorum bono providendi.

Can. 1330, 2°. Debet parochus:
Peculiari omnino studio, praesertim, si nihil obsit, Quadragesimae tempore, pueros sic instituere ut sancte Sancta primum de altari libent.

The obligation of parents to provide for the religious and moral education of their children is founded on both the natural and the positive divine laws.[1] The writer is concerned only with the religious and moral upbringing of the children insofar as it pertains to the preparation for the reception of first Holy Communion. By moral education is understood the proper cultivation of the intellect and of the will. By religious education is implied the needed preparation for the reception of the sacraments, the imparting of catechetical instruction, and the training in one's faith under Catholic influence.[2]

The obligation of providing a proper religious and moral education for their offspring binds the parents of both legitimate and illegitimate children. Parents are in nature the progenitors of their children, and consequently are bound by the natural law to rear them

[1] Coronata, *Institutiones Iuris Canonici,* II, 254; Cocchi, *Commentarium in Codicem,* VI, 47; De Meester, *Juris Canonici et Juris Canonico-Civilis Compendium* (ed. nova, 3 vols. in 4, Brugis: Desclée, 1921-1928), III, 196 (hereafter cited *Compendium*).

[2] Payen, *De Matrimonio in Missionibus* (3 vols., Vol. II, ed. altera, Zi-ka-wei: In typographia T'ou-se-we, 1936), II, 466 and 470.

properly, whether they were born within or outside the bond of lawful wedlock. Not only the parents and those who take the place of parents, such as teachers or guardians, but also the head of the household and the godparents, are bound to see that those who are subject to them receive catechetical instruction.[3]

The obligation of parents and of those mentioned in canon 1335 is not to be understood as meaning that they themselves must undertake the religious instruction of the children for whom they are responsible. They are bound only to provide (*curare*) for the proper religious education of their charges. The Church enjoys the proper and predominant right in all matters which pertain to the spiritual upbringing of children. This right is not an exclusive right, but is rather to be regarded as cumulative with that of the parents. Parents may be regarded as the natural ministers of the Church in this matter.[4] By allowing the Church through her ministers to take care of the religious education of their children, parents fulfill the obligation imposed upon them.

It is the proper and most grave duty of the pastors of souls especially to provide for the catechetical instruction of the people who profess themselves as Christians.[5] Quasi-pastors,[6] parochial administrators,[7] parochial substitute vicars,[8] parochial adjutant priests,[9] and parochial assistant priests[10] have in this matter a like obligation, concurrent with that of pastors, though in its exercise and fulfillment some of the persons here mentioned must undertake their work under the guidance and moderation of the pastor.

There is no conflict between the rights and duties of parents and pastors as regards the religious education of children. The duty of

[3] Canon 1335. Non solum parentes aliique qui parentum locum tenent, sed heri quoque ac patrini obligatione adstringuntur curandi ut omnes sibi subiecti vel commendati catechetica institutione erudiantur.

[4] De Meester, *Compendium,* III, 196.

[5] Canon 1329. Proprium ac gravissimum officium, pastorum praesertim animarum, est catecheticam populi christiani institutionem curare.

[6] Canon 451, § 2, 1°.

[7] Canon 473.

[8] Canon 474.

[9] Canon 475, §§ 1-2.

[10] Canon 476, § 6.

the pastor is to see that children receive such an education. If parents or those who take their place insist on giving this instruction themselves, or on appointing some properly qualified person to do so, the pastor has no right to interfere. The pastor most certainly cannot, under threat of refusing to allow the children to make their first Communion, force parents to send their children to schools of his own choosing or to classes which he personally conducts.[11]

Pastors are required to prepare children with truly exceptional care for the reception of first Holy Communion. This special preparation should take place during Lent if nothing stands in the way.[12] Lent is regarded as the most opportune time for this course of special instruction, inasmuch as it gives an opportunity to all who have reached the age of discretion since the close of the last course of instruction to prepare for the fulfillment of the paschal precept.

It may easily happen that the pastor himself cannot provide for the preparation of the children during Lent for their first Holy Communion, even though the parents are perfectly willing that he should do so. This contingency is provided for by canon 1333, § 1. In virtue of this canon pastors may, and if they are legitimately impeded must, for the religious education of the children, employ the help of other clerics living in the parish, and also, if necessary, of devout lay persons, especially if they belong to the Confraternity of Christian Doctrine or to some similar society established in the parish.

The pastor has the right to demand help from clerics living in his parish. It is his right to call on such clerics whether they be in minor, in major, or in priestly orders. The phrase *"in paroeciae territorio degentium"* is explained as referring to clerics living in their proper parish.[13] Consequently the pastor can require assistance

[11] Cappello, *Summa Iuris Canonici* (3 vols., Vol. II, 3. ed., Romae: apud aedes Universitatis Gregorianae, 1939), II, 88; Wernz-Vidal, *Ius Canonicum,* IV, Pars II, 52.

[12] Canon 1330, 2°. Debet parochus: Peculiari omnino studio, praesertim, si nihil obsit, Quadragesimae tempore, pueros sic instituere ut sancte Sancta primum de altari libent.

[13] Vermeersch-Creusen, *Epitome Iuris Canonici,* II, 410; Cappello, *Summa Iuris Canonici,* II, 89.

only from those clerics who have a domicile or a quasi-domicile in his parish, or from clerics who have no parochial or quasi-parochial domicile elsewhere the while they reside in his parish.[14] Furthermore, the Confraternity of Christian Doctrine should be established in every parish,[15] and thus the pastor becomes enabled to seek help from the members of this Confraternity. Where such a Confraternity is not yet established, help may be sought from the members of similar Catholic Action groups, such as the Confraternity of the Blessed Sacrament, whether the membership consists of men or of women.[16] The provisions of canon 1334 do not apply to the instruction of children.[17]

The Code does not specify the duration of this special course of instruction. Neither does it state how long each instruction should last. Episcopal, synodal or conciliar decrees which determine the duration of the preparation for first Communion must be observed in the localities for which they have been made.[18] In the Province of Portland, Oregon, pastors are required to instruct children in preparation for their first Communion for a period of one month during the paschal season or at some other suitable time on each day when school is held.[19] In other parts of the United States, where no subsequent synodal or episcopal decrees are in force, the law of the III Plenary Council of Baltimore (1884), which requires the priests having the care of souls to instruct candidates for first Com-

[14] Canon 94, §§ 1-2.

[15] Canon 711.

[16] S. C. Conc., decr. *"Provido sane,"* 12 ian. 1935—*AAS,* XXVII (1935), 145-152.

[17] Vermeersch-Creusen, *op. cit.,* II, 410-411; Cappello, *op. cit.,* II, 90.

[18] Cocchi, *Commentarium in Codicem,* VI, 42; Vermeersch-Creusen, *op. cit.,* II, 419; Ferreres, *Institutiones Canonicae* (2 vols., Vol. II, ed. altera, Barcinone: Ex Typis Eugenii Subirana, 1920), II, 117; Sipos, *Enchiridion Iuris Canonici* (Pécs: ex Typographis "Haladás R.T.," 1926), p. 690.

[19] Decr. 32, 2°—*Acta et Decreta Concilii Provincialis Portlandensis in Oregon Quarti anno MCMXXXII* (Portland: Sentinel Printery, 1932), p. 42.

munion three times weekly for a period of at least six weeks,[20] seems to retain its force, since it is not opposed to the canons of the Code.[21]

The preparation of children for first Communion may be combined with their preparation for the reception of the sacraments of penance and confirmation. Children must be prepared for the reception of the Eucharist and for the gaining of sacramental absolution each year, but their preparation for the sacrament of confirmation need be undertaken only in the years when this sacrament is being conferred in the parish.[22]

The reception of Holy Communion by those who have not yet been confirmed is without doubt licit. But it is more commendable and even more conformable to the nature and effects of the sacrament of confirmation, which is the complement of baptism, that children be confirmed before approaching the Holy Table for the first time. However, it is the mind of the Sacred Congregation of the Sacraments that children should not be denied the opportunity of receiving Holy Communion when they have had no opportunity of receiving the sacrament of confirmation.[23]

It has already been shown that children who have reached the years of discretion are bound by the paschal precept irrespective of the completion of non-completion of their seventh year. The pastor

[20] N. 218: "Iubemus ergo ut parvulorum curam assiduam habeant animarum rectores, praesertim quo tempore parantur ad sacram synaxim prima vice recipiendam, et quidem ut ipsimet rectores vel eorum vicarii praedictos parvulos saltem per sex hebdomadas et ter in unaquaque hebdomada (saltem in loco ubi resident vel ad quem facilius accedere possunt), catechismum doceant. . . ." —*Acta et Decreta Concilii Plenarii Baltimorensis Tertii* (Baltimore: John Murphy, 1886), p. 119.

[21] Canon 6. Codex vigentem huc usque disciplinam plerumque retinet, licet opportunas immutationes afferat. Itaque: 1°. Leges quaelibet, sive universales sive particulares, praescriptis huius Codicis oppositae, abrogantur, nisi de particularibus legibus aliud expresse caveatur; . . .

[22] Cf. Coronata, *Tractatus Canonicus de Sacramentis,* II, 254; Cappello, *Summa Iuris Canonici,* II, 88.

[23] S. C. de Sacramentis, resp. 30 iun. 1932: ". . . non tamen iidem censendi sunt prohiberi quominus ad eamdem Mensam prius admittantur, si ad annos discretionis pervenerint, quamvis Confirmationis sacramentum antea accipere non potuerunt."—*AAS,* XXIV (1932), 272; Bouscaren, *The Canon Law Digest,* I, 349.

should so time the preparatory instructions that the greatest possible number of children receive the opportunity of preparing to fulfill the obligation of paschal Communion. If the instructions are given during Lent this end is achieved.

But what if the instructions are given some months before Lent? Is the pastor obliged to prepare a second class of children who have attained the use of reason between the completion of the first course of instruction and the beginning of Lent? The opinion of the writer is that the pastor is bound to undertake this second series of instructions. The reason is obvious. Since children who have reached the age of discretion are bound by the paschal precept, they have the right to receive the due preparation which will enable them to fulfill their obligation. Consequently the pastor should always provide instruction during the Lenten season. If he is unable to do so, he has the right and the obligation to seek the assistance of others.[24]

From the viewpoint of strict law, the pastor fulfills his duty if he provides instruction for the children each year during Lent. Nevertheless it seems more in harmony with the spirit of the law to prepare children for the reception of Holy Communion as soon as they have reached the age of discretion. According to Schathoelter, Pope Pius X taught that children were obliged to receive Holy Communion soon after attaining the use of reason, and that it was not allowable for them to wait over a lengthy period until Eastertime to make their first Communion.[25] No such incumbent obligation can be read into the law as found in the Code.[26]

One of the main reasons why the practice of deferring the reception of first Communion until a comparatively advanced age stand condemned was the danger of the loss of first innocence from the lack of spiritual nourishment. The same reason urges that children be communicated soon after attaining the use of reason. When they attain the use of reason children become capable of sinning, and it is imperative that every means to help them resist temptation be given to them. The ideal practice would consist in preparing each

[24] Cf. *supra*, pp. 75 ff.

[25] "First Communion and the Duty of the Confessor"—*AER*, XXXXVI (1912), 478.

[26] Cf. *supra*, pp. 48 ff.

individual child for first Communion when it reached the age of discretion, so that its first Communion would not be deferred until the following Lent.

But in most parishes it would be impossible for the pastor to provide special instruction for each individual child, and consequently the Code has imposed no obligation that he should do so. It should not, however, be too difficult to arrange a course of instruction two or three times a year. Should parents or other competent persons offer to undertake the preparation of individual children at various times during the year, the pastor should encourage them to do so and then perform his duty according to canon 854, § 5, by taking care that properly instructed children are admitted to Holy Communion as soon as possible.[27]

The object of the special instruction for first Communion should be to prepare both the minds and the hearts of the children for the fruitful reception of the Eucharist. It would be erroneous to assume that the mere dry explanation of the catechism suffices to prepare children properly. The Code requires that children be prepared in such a manner that they will make their first Communion piously (*sancte*).[28] Consequently the instructor should not only teach doctrine, but also, excite in his pupils a deep reverence for the Blessed Sacrament, and thus make them less unworthy of the great privilege of receiving the Body and Blood of Christ.[29] The catechetical instructions should be interwoven with exhortations and precepts calculated to arouse pious affections in the souls of the children.[30]

Children should be taught how to deport themselves when receiving Holy Communion. They should be instructed how to join hands and how to genuflect reverently. It is a commendable practice to use

[27] Parocho autem est officium . . . curandi ut usum rationis assecuti et sufficienter dispositi quamprimum hoc divino cibo reficiantur.

[28] Canon 1330, 2°.

[29] Pius X, litt. *"Inter multa,"* 12 ian. 1905—*Catechetical Documents of Pope Pius X,* translated and edited by Joseph B. Collins (Paterson: St. Anthony Guild Press, 1946), p. 114.

[30] Pius X, litt. encycl. *"Acerbo nimis,"* 15 apr. 1905, N. III: ". . . aptis praeceptionibus et hortationibus adolescentulos et adolescentulas sic instruant, ut sancte sancta primum de altari libent."—*Fontes,* n. 666.

unconsecrated hosts when teaching them the correct position of the head, mouth and tongue in the act of receiving the Sacred Host. The use of such unconsecrated hosts accustoms them to the taste of unleavened bread, and may be the means of preventing gagging and choking on the day they first receive the Eucharist. This practice may also serve to illustrate in a practical way the fact that the difference between the Eucharist and common bread does not depend on the shape or on the taste of the host, and that, in fact, the hosts constitute nothing but common bread before the sacred words of consecration are pronounced over them. An explanation of the reason which motivates this external reverence will help the children to receive with greater interior devotion.

Article 2. The Obligation of Seeing that Children Make Their First Holy Communion

Can. 860. Obligatio praecepti communionis sumendae, quae impuberes gravat, in eos quoque ac praecipue recidit, qui ipsorum curam habere debent, idest in parentes, tutores, confessarium, institutores et parochum.

Can. 854, § 5. Parocho autem est officium advigilandi, etiam per examen, si opportunum prudenter iudicaverit, ne pueri ad sacram Synaxim accedant ante adeptum usum rationis vel sine sufficienti dispositione; itemque curandi ut usum rationis assecuti et sufficienter dispositi quamprimum hoc divino cibo reficiantur.

All those who are entrusted with the care of children have the duty of seeing that their charges satisfy the precept of Paschal Communion. The writer is concerned with this obligation insofar as the fulfilling of this precept coincides with the reception of first Holy Communion.

Canon 860 names in the following order those who are obliged to see that children receive Holy Communion during the paschal season: Parents, guardians, the confessor, teachers and the pastor.

This order is not arbitrarily arranged; it is based on a definite principle of responsibility.[81]

Parents are primarily responsible for the fulfilling of the precept of paschal Communion by their children. Guardians are those who have been appointed by law or by the will of the parents to take care of the children.[82] They have the same rights and duties as parents as far as the spiritual and temporal upbringing of the children entrusted to their care is concerned. Should parents or guardians fail to discharge their duty, the confessor to whom the child penitent goes for absolution is bound to reveal to it its obligation and to urge its fulfillment. Teachers enjoy a delegated right and duty in this respect to be exercised in the name of and by the authority of the father.[83] The pastor, as the spiritual father of the Catholics committed to his care, is bound to warn parents of their obligation in the matter, and, if they fail to act, he should himself induce the child to receive.[84]

From its very nature it is obvious that the duty of seeing that children fulfill the precept of paschal Communion binds the above mentioned persons *in solidum*, that is, in such a way that the obligation incumbent on each ceases when one or the other succeeds in persuading the child to receive Holy Communion during the paschal season. The duty of urging children to satisfy the paschal precept is a grave one, so that any wilful neglect on the part of those who are responsible would result in the commission of a mortal sin.

Children should not be forced to fulfill the precept of paschal Communion. If children who do not wish to receive Holy Communion are forced to do so, there is grave danger that they receive unfruitfully or even sacrilegiously. They should rather be urged and exhorted to approach the altar, and the final decision should be left to the children themselves.[85]

[81] Clinton, *The Paschal Precept*, The Catholic University of America Canon Law Studies no. 73 (Washington, D. C.: The Catholic University of America, 1932), p. 60.

[82] Cappello, *De Sacramentis*, I, 460.

[83] Cappello, *op. cit.*, I, 461.

[84] Cf. De Meester, *Compendium*, I, 277.

[85] Cf. Ayrinhac, *Legislation on the Sacraments*, p. 168; Coronata, *Tractatus Canonicus de Sacramentis*, I, 292.

The pastor has the additional duty of taking care that children who are sufficiently disposed receive the Eucharist as soon as possible.[86] The adverb *"quamprimum"* should be interpreted broadly to mean "without notable delay." [87] Blat states that a notable delay would be present if the pastor were to defer the reception of Holy Communion beyond the paschal season.[88] From this statement it could be inferred that, if the pastor takes care that a child receive at Eastertime, he fulfills the duty imposed on him by canon 854, § 5. This interpretation of the word *"quamprimum"* destroys the force of the last clause of the canon cited. If the duty of seeing that children receive the Eucharist as soon as possible after they have become qualified to do so is identical simply with the duty of seeing that they receive at paschal time, then the last clause of canon 854, § 5, is superfluous, since the latter duty is imposed on the pastor by canon 860. The true meaning of *"quamprimum"* can be understood only if one recalls that compliance with the spirit of the law demands that children be prepared to communicate immediately after attaining the use of reason. The last clause of canon 854, § 5, refers to the duty of the pastor to take care that such children receive Holy Communion soon after becoming qualified to do so. Cappello more correctly understood the force of the clause when he interpreted it as meaning "within one or two months under ordinary circumstances." [89]

Article 3. The Competence to Judge of the Child's Fitness for Admission to First Holy Communion

Can. 854, § 4. De sufficienti puerorum dispositione ad primam communionem iudicium esto sacerdoti a confessionibus eorumque parentibus aut iis qui loco parentum sunt.

[86] Canon 854, § 5. Parocho autem est officium . . . curandi ut usum rationis assecuti et sufficienter dispositi quamprimum hoc divino cibo reficiantur.

[87] Fanfani, *De Iure Parochorum,* p. 257; Ayrinhac, *op. cit.,* p. 167; Blat, *De Sacramentis,* pp. 184-185.

[88] *Loc. cit.*

[89] *De Sacramentis,* I, 456.

§ 5. Parocho autem est officium advigilandi, etiam per examen, si opportunum prudenter iudicaverit, ne pueri ad sacram Synaxim accedant ante adeptum usum rationis vel sine sufficienti dispositione . . .

The word "right" (*ius*) is not found either in the Code or in the decree *Quam singulari* to describe the duty and the office of those who can judge a child's fitness for admission to first Holy Communion. Strictly taken, there is no question of right as applying either to the parents, or to the confessor, or also to the pastor. A right exists only as it regards the child. For this reason Cappello prefers not to use the word "right" when he discusses those to whom it pertains to judge of a child's dispositions for admitting it to first Communion.[40]

The Code does not explicitly state whose prerogative it is to admit children to Holy Communion. It merely states that it belongs to the confessor and to the parents, or to those who take the place of the parents, to pass judgment on the sufficiency of the child's dispositions.[41] It is necessary to refer to the decree *Quam singulari* for any explicit mention of the competence for admitting children to their first Communion. The pertinent norm of this decree states that it pertains to the father, or to those who take the place of the father, and to the confessor to admit a child to first Holy Communion.[42]

Cappello asserts that it is necessary to distinguish between the power to judge and the competence to admit, and complains that many authors fail to do so. It is difficult to determine what precisely he means when he speaks of the admission of children to Holy Communion. On the one hand he claims that the confessor and the parents enjoy the competence to admit them, and on the other hand he seems to introduce the idea of the right to *give* Holy Communion when he says that the pastor has not the right to forbid a child

[40] *De Sacramentis,* I, 459.

[41] Canon 854, § 4.

[42] N. IV: ". . . Ad patrem vero, aut ad illos qui vices eius gerunt, et ad confessarium, secundum Catechismum Romanum, pertinet admittere puerum ad primam Communionem."—*AAS,* II (1910), 582; *Fontes,* n. 2103.

to communicate in a non-parochial church.[43] There simply cannot be any debatable question regarding any competence on the part of parents to give Holy Communion to their child.[44] Cappello's insistence on the necessity of differentiating between the competence for judging the children's fitness and for admitting them to the sacred table may be due to his apparent misconception of the nature of the competence regarding their admission to the reception of Holy Communion.

The writer understands by the latter prerogative the moral power to give or to refuse a child permission to receive first Holy Communion. Theoretically there is a distinction between the competence to judge a child's dispositions and the prerogative to give it permission to approach the altar. In practice this distinction is of little importance. The two points of competence are so closely connected and so mutually dependent that the writer has thought it best to discuss both in the present article.

The result of the judgment of the child's dispositions is the foundation on which rests the decision to admit or to debar it from first Holy Communion. Consequently both powers pertain to the same persons, namely to the parents or to those who take their place and also to the confessor. In the last analysis the competence to admit the child is simply the capacity for implementing the result of the judgment regarding its dispositions. The decree *Quam singulari* states that, according to the Roman Catechism, it is the parents and the confessor who should admit a child to its first Communion. The Roman Catechism declared that no one can better judge the age at which a child should be admitted to Holy Communion than the father and the priest to whom it confesses its sins. To these persons it pertains to find out whether the child has acquired a knowledge of and a taste for this sacrament.[45] The text of the Roman Catechism

[43] *Op. cit.*, I, 455-456.

[44] The ordinary minister of Holy Communion is the priest, and the extraordinary minister is the deacon. Cf. canon 845, §§ 1-2.

[45] Pars II, *De Eucharistiae Sacramento*, n. 63: "Qua vero aetate pueris sacra mysteria danda sint, nemo melius constituere poterit, quam pater et sacerdos, cui illi confitentur peccata; ad illos enim pertinet explorare, et a pueris percunctari, an huius admirabilis sacramenti cognitionem aliquam acceperint, et gustum habeant."—*Catechismus Concilii Tridentini*, p. 226.

taken in conjunction with N. IV of the decree *Quam singulari* [46] illustrates the intimate connection and interdependence of the competence to judge a child's dispositions and the prerogative to give it permission to approach the altar.

There is no necessity, then, for insisting overmuch on the distinction between the two points of competence. Both pertain to the same persons. The prerogative to admit children to their first Communion is nothing more than the complement of the acknowledged competence to judge their dispositions. The Code makes no explicit mention of the competence to admit children. Yet this omission cannot rightly be regarded as an oversight on the part of the legislator. By explicitly acknowledging to the confessor and the parents the competence to judge and discern the dispositions of the children the Code implicitly confirms their prerogative to admit the children, which prerogative was explicitly recognized and established as theirs in the decree *Quam singulari*.

The question now arises: Is the consent both of the parents and of the confessor necessary before a child can approach the altar? It is clear from the decree *Quam singulari* that the competence for admitting a child to its first Holy Communion belongs both to the parents and to the confessor.[47] It is of course desirable that the confessor and the parents act together in the matter, but in a case of disagreement any one of them can admit the child.[48] It follows from this that the confessor and the parents alike are equally competent in the matter of judging a child's dispositions. The prerogative to admit a child is founded on the acknowledged competence to judge its dispositions, and consequently any difference of opinion as to whether a child should or should not be admitted must be based

[46] Cf. footnote 42 of this article.

[47] N. V.: "Semel aut pluries in anno curent parochi indicere atque habere Communionem generalem puerorum ad eamque, non modo novensiles admittere, sed etiam alios, qui *parentum confessariive* consensu, ut supra dictum est, iam antea primitus de altari sancta libarunt."—*AAS,* II (1910), 582; *Fontes,* n. 2103. Italics inserted by the writer.

[48] Cf. O'Donnell, "The Admission of Children to Holy Communion"—*IER,* 5. series, III (1914), 82; Vermeersch, "De Primae Communionis Aetate,"—*Periodica,* V (1913), 176; Zulueta, "The Control of Childrens' First Communions"—*AER,* XLVIII (1913), 24.

on the divergent judgments as to its dispositions. The particle—*que,* as found in canon 854, § 4, must be understood in a disjunctive, and not in a conjunctive, sense. Cappello [49] and Coronata [50] correctly interpret it as having a disjunctive force.

The decree *Quam singulari* makes prior mention of the parents or of those who take the place of parents, and subsequent mention of the confessor, as enjoying the prerogative of admitting children to their first Holy Communion. The Code mentions the confessor first, and then the parents or those who take the place of parents, when it deals with the point of competence for judging and discerning the dispositions of a child. This reversal of the order of the persons mentioned can be explained if one properly attends to the particular purpose of the decree *Quam singulari* and the particular aim of canon 854, § 4. The object of the former was to vindicate the right of children who had reached the age of discretion to receive Holy Communion. Parents or those who take the place of parents were through their daily contact with the child the best qualified persons to judge whether or not it possessed the use of reason. The Code, on the other hand, deals with the intellectual and moral dispositions of the child in the canon just cited. [51] The confessor is the best qualified person to judge whether a child possesses these dispositions, for to him alone are revealed the innermost secrets of the child's soul.

From the foregoing discussion it must not be concluded that the prerogative to admit the child belongs *exclusively* to the parents and to the confessor. In certain circumstances the pastor may also have the power to give or to refuse the child permission to communicate. The writer is not here contemplating or referring to the fact that the pastor has the same competence inasmuch as he is at the same time the confessor to whom the child-penitent goes for sacramental absolution. In this case the pastor enjoys the authority to admit the child not by virtue of his office as pastor but in view of his office as confessor.

[49] *De Sacramentis,* I, 456.

[50] *Tractatus Canonicus de Sacramentis,* I, 292.

[51] From canon 854, § 5, it is evident that when the Code uses the word *"dispositiones"* it refers to the moral and intellectual qualifications of the child, and not to its possession of the use of reason.

In virtue of his pastoral office the pastor has the duty of warning parents of their obligation to induce their children, if they are properly qualified, to communicate during the paschal season. If they fail to perform their duty, he should himself induce the child to receive. In such circumstances the pastor could give a child permission to approach the altar. Again, in virtue of his rightful power to exercise vigilance over the admission of children to Holy Communion the pastor may be obliged to veto the decision made by the parents.[52] The co-ordination of the power of vigilance on the part of the pastor with the prerogative of admitting the child as it pertains to the parents and to the confessor is discussed in the following paragraphs.

Authors agree that the power of the pastor to exercise vigilance is a power of a very general nature, and that it cannot be interpreted as meaning that the pastor has the power to interfere at will with the decisions of the parents or of the confessor. He cannot require all the children of his parish to submit to an examination as a prerequisite for their admission to first Holy Communion. The power of vigilance can be exercised only when there is present a well founded doubt concerning the dispositions of a particular child.[53] Unfortunately this general consensus does not answer all the questions connected with the problem of co-ordinating the prerogative regarding the child's admission with the power of vigilance regarding the same point. It does not decide, for example, what constitutes undue interference with the prerogative of the parents and of the confessor.

Coronata insists that the prerogative to admit children to their first Holy Communion belongs absolutely to the parents, and that consequently the pastor can never interfere with their decision. He concludes that the pastor can exercise the power of vigilance in only such cases wherein a child comes to receive the Eucharist without

[52] Canon 854, § 5. Parocho autem est officium advigilandi, etiam per examen, si opportunum prudenter iudicaverit, ne pueri ad sacram Synaxim accedant ante adeptum usum rationis vel sine sufficienti dispositione; . . .

[53] Cf. De Meester, *Compendium,* I, 277; Ayrinhac, *Legislation on the Sacraments,* p. 167; Cappello, *De Sacramentis,* I, 456; Vermeersch-Creusen, *Epitome Iuris Canonici,* II, 71; Regatillo, *Ius Sacramentarium,* I, 178.

having obtained the permission of its parents, of its teachers or guardians, or of the confessor.[54] This theory, though it certainly indicates a way for obviating all undue interference on the part of the pastor, is nevertheless not a wholly satisfactory one. Its application could open the way for many abuses. Parents are naturally desirous that their children be regarded as being at least equally intelligent with the children of their neighbors. If it should happen that a particular child is rather tardy in its intellectual development, there is present a grave temptation for the parents to conceal its mental deficiency from others by inducing it to approach the altar along with the children of a normal intelligence who are its equal in age. The pastor, even though he knew of the child's lack of proper dispositions, would be powerless to prevent its receiving the Eucharist. Coronata's theory can hardly be defended on the ground that the lack of the confessor's consent would then act as a check on the parents, for he correctly teaches that either the parents or the confessor are competent in permitting the child to receive its first Holy Communion.[55] Consequently this method of reconciling the power of vigilance with the prerogative of admitting the child to Holy Communion is not acceptable to the writer.

It is more reasonable to hold that, whenever the pastor has a well founded motive for doubting the sufficiency of a child's dispositions, he has the power to demand an examination, if his prudent judgment so dictates, even though the child has received permission from the parents or the confessor to receive. The fact that the suspicion of the existence of some irregularity must be well founded prevents undue interference with the decision of the parents or of the confessor. If both the parents and the confessor agree that a particular child should be admitted to first Holy Communion, it is almost impossible to visualize a well founded doubt as to its qualifications. Should the parents and the confessor disagree, then the presence of such a well founded doubt seems indicated as at least probable, especially if the decision of the confessor is that the child should not yet be admitted to its first Holy Communion. Cappello

[54] *Tractatus Canonicus de Sacramentis,* I, 292.

[55] *Loc. cit.*

teaches that when the confessor gives a child permission to approach the altar there can scarcely be present any reasonable doubt as to the sufficiency of its qualifications.[56]

Ordinarily the parents of a child will be satisfied to allow the pastor to make the final decision whether or not it should be allowed to receive the Eucharist. But, what if a disagreement arises between the pastor and the parents, or between the pastor and the confessor? If the pastor legitimately intervenes in a particular case and thereupon decides that the child is not properly qualified for admission to its first Holy Communion, must his ruling be obeyed?

Cappello,[57] Vermeersch-Creusen [58] and Regatillo [59] assert that, strictly in accord with the warrant of the law, the parents are not bound to stand by his decision. On the other hand, the legislation of the Provincial Council of Malines (1920) seems rather to have indicated that the decision of the pastor was to be regarded as final in the case wherein he had examined a child in view of some reasonable doubt as to its dispositions.[60] The problem could well be solved by having the child communicate in some church outside the pastor's jurisdiction. But what if the parents or the confessor wish it to make its first Communion in the parish church?

The solution of the possible dispute as existing between the pastor and the parents will first be attempted. It must be borne in mind that the enjoyment of the use of reason and the possession of the dispositions discussed in the preceding chapter are distinct though necessary qualifications for admission to Holy Communion. If the pastor maintains that a child should not be admitted to the altar since it does not possess the use of reason, but the parents insist that it has attained the years of discretion, it seems that the decision of the parents should stand. The parents or those who take the place of the parents are best qualified to decide whether or not a child enjoys the use of reason in view of their daily contact with the child. But if the dispute centers on whether or not a particular child

[56] *De Sacramentis,* I, 456.

[57] *Loc. cit.*

[58] *Epitome Iuris Canonici,* II, 71.

[59] *Ius Sacramentarium,* I, 178.

[60] Art. 188—as cited by Vermeersch-Creusen, *op. cit.*, II, 71, footnote 1.

possesses the necessary dispositions for admission to Holy Communion, then the decision of the pastor should be upheld. The pastor in virtue of his office as teacher [61] and in consequence of his authorized status as dispenser of the sacraments is best qualified to decide whether the required intellectual and moral dispositions are present in the child.

It may be objected that the alleged possession of the use of reason can never be the subject of dispute between the pastor and the parents inasmuch as the use of reason is a necessary condition for the acquiring of the requisite dispositions for admission to the reception of the Eucharist. In answer to this objection it is sufficient to point out that a child which does not enjoy a sufficient use of reason may *apparently* possess the required spiritual and intellectual dispositions. While admitting upon the examination of the child that it appeared to possess a sufficient knowledge and devotion, the pastor could nevertheless claim that the child really did not understand or appreciate in any way the meaning of its answers, in short, that it did not possess the use of reason. Should the parents assert that the child did possess the use of reason, then the pastor has no option but to allow it to communicate.

It has already been noted that when the confessor gives a child permission to approach the altar there can scarcely be any reasonable doubt as to its qualifications. The confessor by reason of his office has a unique opportunity of testing both the existence of the use of reason and the possession of the required dispositions in a child-penitent. Because of his theological training he is as well qualified as the pastor to judge the dispositions of a child. Again, his questioning of the child will reveal whether it possesses the use of reason.

An additional reason which should compel the pastor to hesitate in questioning the confessor's decision is the danger that any direct questioning of the confessor might result in a direct or an indirect violation of the seal of confession.[62] The confessor should follow the

[61] Cf. canons 1329 and 1330, 1°-2°.

[62] Canon 2368, § 1, specifies the penalties which should be inflicted on a confessor who indirectly violates the seal of confession. A confessor who directly breaks the seal of confession by that very fact incurs the penalty of excommunication which is reserved to the Holy See in the most special manner. —Cf. canon 2369, § 1.

practice of merely telling the child of his decision, and then have the child report that decision to its parents. He should not directly discuss the matter with the parents or with the pastor. Should the pastor wish to question the confessor's decision which admits the child to its first Communion, then he should do so through the child. But it is obvious that even this practice is not always to be recommended, since it may leave the child under the impression that the pastor is trying to find out everything that passed between it and its confessor. All things considered, it is best for the pastor never to question the decision which a confessor renders regarding the fitness of a child who is a candidate for first Holy Communion.

The parents or the confessor are under no obligation to tell the pastor that they intend admitting a child to first Holy Communion, though it is advisable that they do so. In virtue of his obligation to exercise vigilance the pastor can legitimately make inquiry in order to find out which children are to be admitted. The ideal which should be aimed at by the parents, the confessor and the pastor is the fullest possible mutual co-operation.

If a child publicly approaches the altar rail, the pastor cannot refuse it Holy Communion for the mere reason that he doubts the sufficiency of its dispositions. To refuse a child Holy Communion under such circumstances would be to treat it as a sinner or as an unworthy person.[63] Cappello[64] and Vermeersch-Creusen[65] state that in this case the pastor could gently and suavely attempt to persuade it not to receive. But if there is any likelihood that such an attempt would embarass the child or create in it an aversion for the Sacrament, then the pastor should allow it to receive. But if it is altogether certain that a child which presents itself at the altar rail could not possess the use of reason or the necessary dispositions, then the pastor could legitimately abstain from communicating it. Thus there is no obligation to communicate a child which could not possibly possess the required qualifications in view of its very tender age.

In consideration of the rather involved discussion regarding, on

[63] Cf. canon 855, § 1.

[64] *De Sacramentis,* I, 457.

[65] *Epitome Iuris Canonici,* II, 71.

the one hand, the parents' and the confessor's prerogative to admit children to their first Communion and, on the other hand, the pastor's warranted power of vigilance against admitting children who lack the needed dispositions, the writer has thought it best to conclude this article with a brief summation of the salient points of the discussion: (1) The competent power to admit children to their first Holy Communion is in the last analysis simply the competence to implement the judgment regarding their needed dispositions. (2) The prerogative which entitles both the parents and the confessor to admit the children to the first reception of the Eucharist is not an altogether exclusive possession of theirs. (3) The pastor can legitimately exercise his power to debar an insufficiently disposed child from the reception of first Holy Communion irrespective of the circumstance that the parents have or have not given it permission to receive. (4) Theoretically the pastor has the power to veto the confessor's decision which favors the admission of the child. In practice the safer course is that the decision of the confessor be honored without question.

Article 4. Obligations of the Pastor upon the Child's Reception of First Holy Communion

Can. 1331. Praeter puerorum institutionem de qua in can. 1330, parochus non omittat pueros, qui primam communionem recenter receperint, uberius ac perfectius catechismo excolere.

Can. 470, § 1. Habeat parochus libros paroeciales, idest librum baptizatorum, confirmatorum, matrimoniorum, defunctorum; etiam librum de statu animarum accurate conficere pro viribus curet; et omnes hos libros, secundum usum ab Ecclesia probatum vel a proprio Ordinario praescriptum, conscribat ac diligenter asservet.

Canon 1331 imposes on the pastor the obligation of providing a fuller and more perfect catechetical instruction for the children who have received their first Holy Communion. In the preceding chapter it was shown that what is necessary for admission to Holy Communion outside the danger of death is simply a rudimentary knowledge of the articles of faith absolutely necessary for salvation, in addition to a knowledge of what the Eucharist is. An even lesser intellectual preparation suffices for the reception of Viaticum. But the Church is not content to allow children to grow up without the opportunity of learning more about their faith, and hence she insists that they receive a more thorough schooling in Christian doctrine.

It is possible that the pastor may foresee that children will not return for this more detailed instruction after they have received their first Holy Communion. But even the strong probability of such an eventuality cannot be used as an excuse for deferring the reception of the Eucharist.

The advantage of a more solid grounding in doctrine is more than offset by the possible disadvantage—the loss of baptismal innocence—which can be effectively obviated through the reception of Holy Communion at an earlier time. In the year 1884 the Bishop of Annecy ruled that attendance at catechism classes for the two preceding years was a necessary condition for admission to first Holy Communion. The object of the bishop in promulgating this decree was to keep the children longer in the schools, and thus to assure them of a more solid grounding in Catholic doctrine. A pastor of the diocese of Annecy brought the decree to the attention of the Holy See. As a result of his action the Sacred Congregation of the Council declared that this condition bound only with regard to the public and solemn reception of Holy Communion: the bishop could not prohibit pastors from admitting privately to Holy Communion children who had reached the age of discretion.[66]

The Code does not explicitly mention that the pastor is to record the names of those who have received first Communion when it enumerates the parochial books which the pastor is obliged to maintain.[67] The duty of compiling such a record is however im-

[66] Cf. *Thesaurus,* CXLVII (1888), 474-487; *Le Canoniste Contemporain,* XII (1889), 154.

[67] Explicit mention of the obligation to keep such a record is found in Decr. 145 of the IV Provincial Council of Portland, Oregon (1932)—*Acta et Decreta Concilii Provincialis Portlandensis in Oregon Quarti,* p. 70.

plicitly contained in the obligation of keeping a record which shows the state of souls in a parish.[68] The pastor is not obliged to send a copy of this record to the chancery office, but the ordinary or his delegate may inspect it on the occasion of the diocesan visitation or at any other opportune time.[69]

In addition to showing whether those who have reached the use of reason have fulfilled their obligation of receiving Holy Communion, such a record may supply valuable information in matrimonial cases in which the validity of a marriage is impugned in view of the alleged fact that the requisite juridical form for the contraction of the marriage was not observed.[70]

[68] Cf. canon 470, § 1.

[69] Canon 470, §§ 3-4.

[70] Cf. Doheny, *Canonical Procedure in Matrimonial Cases* (2 vols., Vol. II, Milwaukee: The Bruce Publishing Company, 1944), II, 584.

CHAPTER VI

ABNORMAL PERSONS

Can. 88, § 3. Impubes, ante plenum septennium, dicitur infans seu puer vel parvulus et censetur non sui compos; expleto autem septennio, usum rationis habere praesumitur. Infanti assimilantur quotquot usu rationis sunt habitu destituti.

The writer uses the term "abnormal persons" to indicate not only those who are mentally deficient but also those who lack one or more of the faculties of sight, speech or hearing. A discussion regarding the lawfulness of communicating those who are deprived of any or all of these faculties will be found towards the end of this chapter.

It has previously been shown that the recipient of Holy Communion must not only enjoy the use of reason, but in addition must possess certain spiritual and corporeal dispositions. The possession of these qualifications, however, may not at all times warrant the administration of the Eucharist, for the Roman Ritual rules that Holy Communion should not be given when there is danger of irreverence to the Sacred Species.[1]

Irreverence to the Host may arise in various ways. The frenzied state of a sick person, the presence of a persistent cough, or an affliction with some similar malady are potential sources of irreverence to the Host.[2] Other possible sources of irreverence are vomiting and expectoration. A discussion of the proper procedure in case there is present the danger of indignity to the Host from any of the here mentioned causes will be found in the next chapter. It is sufficient

[1] Tit. IV, cap. 1, *de sanctissimo Eucharistiae sacramento*, n. 10: "Amentibus praeterea, seu phreneticis communicare non licet; licebit tamen, si quando habeant lucida intervalla, et devotionem ostendant, dum in eo statu manent, si nullum indignitatis periculum adsit."

[2] *Rituale Romanum*, tit. IV, cap. 4, *de communione infirmorum*, n. 4.

to note here that the Eucharist may not be administered when such danger is encountered. In order to avoid needless repetition the writer wishes it to be understood that when, in the following paragraphs, he states that a certain type of abnormal person may be admitted to Holy Communion, he means that such persons may receive the Eucharist provided that they possess the necessary qualifications and provided that there is not present any danger of irreverence.

Those who have been totally insane from birth may not be admitted to Holy Communion. In law such persons enjoy the standing of children who have not yet attained the years of discretion.[3] Consequently they are prohibited from approaching the altar. It may happen however that a person insane from birth is not totally but only partially insane. A person's insanity may center on some particular object, and as a consequence he may enjoy the outlook of a normal individual on other things. Authors agree that such a person may be allowed to communicate, provided that the special object of his insanity is not the Eucharist.[4] This viewpoint seems quite reasonable, for such an abnormal person may possess all the necessary qualifications for admission to the reception of Holy Communion.

There is no difficulty in treating of the possibility of communicating the insane who enjoy lucid intervals. The *Roman Ritual* explicitly states that such persons may receive Holy Communion during the intervals when their mental disorder has abated.[5]

The question now arises: May the Eucharist ever be administered to an insane person while he is actually suffering from the loss of reason? In other words, does the rubric of the *Roman Ritual*, which prohibits the giving of Holy Communion to the insane except when they actually enjoy a lucid interval, contain an absolute prohibition which admits of no exception? Authors agree that the Eucharist could never be given to an actually insane person outside

[3] Cf. canon 88, § 3.

[4] Gasparri, *De Sanctissima Eucharistia*, II, p. 356, n. 1123; Cappello, *De Sacramentis*, I, 364; Coronata, *Tractatus Canonicus de Sacramentis*, I, 285; Regatillo, *Ius Sacramentarium*, I, 178.

[5] Cf. footnote 1 of this chapter for the pertinent text of the *Roman Ritual*.

the danger of death. Gasparri seems to doubt whether even Viaticum could be administered to such an individual, but he expressly refrains from condemning those who maintain that it is lawful to give Viaticum to a person who is actually insane but who, before losing the use of reason, was properly disposed for Its reception.[6]

No solution to the problem can be deduced from the words of the *Roman Ritual* itself. The revised (1925) edition retains the ruling of the pre-Code edition in identical words.[7] O'Kane-Fallon confess that the rubric in question is somewhat ambiguous, and state that in practice the common teaching of theologians may safely be followed.[8] The consensus of theologians since the time of St. Thomas has been that those who once enjoyed the use of reason and who are actually insane at the time of danger of death may receive Viaticum if, while they were sane, they formed and never revoked at least an implicit intention of receiving the Eucharist.[9] The words of the Catechism of the Council of Trent lend additional weight to the teaching of the theologians. The relevant section of this Catechism states that, if before becoming insane a person had the intention of living a good and religious life, he could receive Viaticum when dying, provided that there was no danger of irreverence.[10] Such an intention contains an implicit intention of receiving Viaticum, and it has already been pointed out that an implicit intention suffices for the fruitful reception of Viaticum.[11]

[6] *Op. cit.*, II, pp. 357-358, n. 1124.

[7] Cf. *supra*, chapter II, footnote 55.

[8] *Notes on the Rubrics of the Roman Ritual*, p. 316.

[9] St. Thomas, *Summa Theologica*, Pars III, q. 80, a. 9; Suarez, *De Eucharistia*, q. 80, art. 9, disp. 68, sec. 6—*Opera Omnia*, XXI, 520; De Lugo, *De Sacramento Eucharistiae*, disp. 13, sect. 3, n. 24—*Disputationes Scholasticae et Morales*, IV, 59; Liguori, *Theologia Moralis*, Lib. VI, *de Eucharistia*, n. 302; Cappello, *De Sacramentis*, I, 364-365; Regatillo, *Ius Sacramentarium*, I, 179; Coronata, *Tractatus Canonicus de Sacramentis*, I, 285; Tanquerey, *Synopsis Theologiae Dogmaticae*, III, 655; Noldin-Schmitt, *Summa Theologiae Moralis*, III, 138.

[10] "Quamvis si antequam in insaniam inciderent, piam et religiosam animi voluntatem praestulerunt, licebit eis in fine vitae, ex concilii Carthaginiensis decreto, eucharistiam adminstrare, modo vomitionis, vel alterius indignitatis et incommodi periculum nullum timendum sit."—*Catechismus Concilii Tridentini*, Pars II, *De Eucharistiae Sacramento*, n. 64.

[11] Cf. *supra*, p. 60.

From the foregoing it is apparent that the rubric of the *Roman Ritual* which forbids the administration of Holy Communion to those who are actually and totally insane, does not contain an absolute prohibition. The Eucharist may be administered by way of Viaticum to an insane person who once enjoyed the use of reason and who, before suffering the loss of sanity, formed at least an implicit intention of receiving Viaticum.

A further class of mentally deficient persons will now be discussed. To this class belong persons who cannot be regarded as really insane, but who nevertheless cannot be regarded as normal persons. They enjoy indeed the use of reason, but in a feeble and vapid manner (*semifatui*). May such persons be admitted to receive Holy Communion? Refusal or permission to approach the altar depends on the presence or absence of the requisite dispositions as enumerated in canon 854, §§ 2-3. When there is question of the fulfillment of the paschal precept or of the reception of Holy Viaticum, it seems equitable to resolve in favor of the individual any doubts regarding the sufficiency of his dispositions, according to the axiom, *"sacramenta propter homines."* [12] Noldin-Schmitt advise that the minister should not be scrupulous in administering the Eucharist in such cases.[13]

The last type of abnormal person considered is that class of persons who lack one or more of the faculties of sight, speech and hearing. Liguori taught that Holy Communion should be refused to those who were born deaf, dumb and blind.[14] Gasparri, adopting the opinion of Liguori, went so far as to assert that in the Latin Church those who have been deaf, dumb and blind from birth are by ecclesiastical law incapable of receiving Holy Communion even though they be instructed.[15] Cappello with good reason takes exception to Gasparri's assertion, and states that if anyone of the

[12] Cf. Vermeersch, *Theologia Moralis*, III, 175.

[13] *Summa Theologiae Moralis*, III, 138.

[14] *Theologia Moralis*, Lib. VI, *de Eucharistia*, n. 303.

[15] "Ex his apparet esse quoque, saltem in Ecclesia Latina, iure ecclesiastico incapaces sacrae communionis . . . surdi-muti-caeci simul a nativitate, licet instituti."—*De Sanctissima Eucharistia*, II, p. 356, n. 1123.

class of persons now under consideration is duly instructed such a person should be allowed to communicate.[16]

It seems impossible to find any legal foundation for Gasparri's opinion. It would be understandable if he had merely stated that such persons could not become properly instructed. But there exists no legal basis for insisting that, even though they be instructed, those who are deaf, dumb and blind from birth should be excluded from Holy Communion. It cannot be urged that the lack of these faculties connotes the absence of the use of reason. Modern methods of instruction have demonstrated the fact that such persons can acquire a considerable amount of intellectual knowledge. When, therefore, it is shown that a deaf, blind and dumb person possesses the requisite qualifications for admission to Holy Communion, there is no apparent reason why he should not be allowed to receive like a normal person. The same rule holds for those who lack one or two of the above mentioned faculties. The ultimate criterion regarding the lawfulness of communicating them is the presence or absence of the dispositions mentioned in canon 854, §§ 2-3.

[16] *De Sacramentis,* I, 366.

CHAPTER VII

FIRST HOLY COMMUNION AS VIATICUM

Can. 854, § 2. In periculo mortis, ut sanctissima Eucharistia pueris ministrari possit ac debeat, satis est ut sciant Corpus Christi a communi cibo discernere illudque reverenter adorare.

The great majority of theologians and canonists agree that men are bound by divine precept to receive Holy Communion when they are in danger of death.[1] The danger of death which urges the reception of Viaticum must not be confused with the danger of death which warrants the administration of the sacrament of extreme unction.[2] The subject of extreme unction must be in danger of death from some intrinsic infirmity—old age may be considered an infirmity—which actually affects him at the time the sacrament is being administered.[3] The danger of death which suffices for the administration of Holy Viaticum may arise from a cause which is intrinsic or extrinsic to the recipient.[4] Thus a con-

[1] Vasquez, disp. 214, cap. 2, nn. 6-10—*Libri Commentariorum in Tertiam Partem S. Thomae,* III, 344; Suarez, *De Eucharistia,* q. 71, art. II, disp. 69, sec. 3, n. 2, in *Opera Omnia,* XXI, 533; De Lugo, *De Sacramento Eucharistiae,* disp. 16, sec. 2, n. 27—*Disputationes Scholasticae et Morales,* IV, 140; Liguori, *Theologia Moralis,* lib. VI, *de Eucharistia,* n. 290; Genicot, *Theologiae Moralis Institutiones,* II, 198; Gasparri, *De Sanctissima Eucharistia,* II, pp. 372-373, nn. 1146-1147; Cappello, *De Sacramentis,* I, 385-386; Prümmer, *Manuale Theologiae Moralis,* III, 155; Merkelbach, *Summa Theologiae Moralis,* III, 242; Sabetti-Barrett, *Compendium Theologiae Moralis,* p. 628; Tanquerey, *Synopsis Theologiae Dogmaticae,* III, 648-649.

[2] Canon 940, § 1. Extrema unctio praeberi non potest nisi fideli, qui post adeptum usum rationis ob infirmitatem vel senium in periculo mortis versetur.

[3] Cf. O'Kane-Fallon, *Notes on the Rubrics of the Roman Ritual,* p. 453.

[4] *Rituale Romanum,* tit. IV, cap. 4, *de communione infirmorum,* n. 1: "In periculo mortis, *quavis ex causa* procedat, fideles sacrae communionis recipiendae praecepto tenentur." (Italics inserted by the writer.)

demned prisoner who enjoys good health could receive Viaticum, but could not receive extreme unction.[5] Moral certitude that death will soon follow, that is, certitude that the subject is *in articulo mortis,* is not required as a necessary condition for the administration of Holy Communion by way of Viaticum. If circumstances are such that a person stands an equal chance of losing his life or of surviving, then he is a fit subject for the reception of Viaticum.[6] Older theologians frequently mentioned the dangers encountered on a protracted voyage as furnishing a sufficient basis for the reception of Holy Communion as Viaticum. At the present time such a trip, whether by boat or by plane, would not necessarily warrant the administration of Viaticum.

The reception of Holy Communion by way of Viaticum does not depend on the will of the subject. The Eucharist must be received as Viaticum whenever the precept to communicate during the danger of death urges.[7] The essential difference between simple Holy Communion and Viaticum lies in the difference of the formulas prescribed by the *Roman Ritual* for the administration of each.[8]

Not infrequently the nature of the malady from which a person suffers when he is in danger of death through sickness poses a problem to the minister of Holy Communion. The Ritual forbids the administration of the Eucharist when indignity to the Sacred

[5] Cf. S. C. de Prop. Fide (C.P. pro Sin.-Tunkin. Occident.), 21 iul. 1841, ad 1 et 2—*Fontes,* n. 4789; *Collect.,* n. 928; S. C. de Prop. Fide (C.P. pro Sin.), 20 febr. 1801—*Fontes,* n. 4662; Collect., n. 651.

[6] D'Annibale (1815-1892) defined the danger of death thus: ". . . illud rerum discrimen, in quo cum quis constitutus est, ipsum, et superesse, et occumbere posse, utrumque est vere graviterque probabile . . ."—*Summula Theologiae Moralis,* I, n. 38.

[7] Cf. Vasquez, disp. 214, cap. 2, n. 17—*op. cit.,* III, 345.

[8] The formula for the administration of simple Holy Communion reads: "Corpus Domini nostri Iesu Christi custodiat animam tuam in vitam aeternam. Amen."—*Rituale Romanum,* tit. IV, cap. 2, *ordo administrandi sacram communionem,* n. 5. The prescribed formula for the administration of Viaticum is: "Accipe, frater (*vel* soror), Viaticum Corporis Domini nostri Iesu Christi, qui te custodiat ab hoste maligno, et perducat in vitam aeternam. Amen."—*Rituale Romanum,* tit. IV, cap. 4, *de communione infirmorum,* n. 19.

Species is feared because of the frenzied state of the patient, or because of a persistent cough, or because of some other similar malady.[9]

Delirium does not of necessity debar a person from the reception of Viaticum. An implicit intention of receiving Holy Communion, deduced from the unconscious person's previous manner of life, suffices for the fruitful reception of this sacrament. It is desirable, however, that Viaticum be administered, if that is possible, while the person is conscious.[10] If, however, it is feared that the patient will not recover consciousness, or that he will be unable to receive the Eucharist when he does regain his senses, Viaticum may be administered without any further delay.

Irreverence to the Host must always be avoided even if this means that an attempt to communicate a dying person cannot be made. Authors recommend the giving of an unconsecrated particle to the sick person in order to determine if any danger of irreverence exist. The minister of Viaticum need have no scruples about making such a test, since the Code expressly exempts all those who are in danger of death from the obligation of observing the law of the natural fast.[11]

The state of frenzy (*ob phrenesim*) mentioned in the Ritual as an impediment to the reception of Viaticum connotes something more than the mere state of delirium. Frenzy is usually understood as a state of mental derangement accompanied with violent physical action. The danger of irreverence to the Host is very frequently present in such cases, as it is often impossible to predict the reactions which may follow the administration of the Eucharist. Con-

[9] Tit. IV, cap. 4, *de communione infirmorum*, n. 4: "Potest quidem Viaticum brevi morituris dari non ieiunis; id tamen diligenter curandum est, ne iis tribuatur, a quibus ob phrenesim, sive ob assiduam tussim, aliumve similem morbum, aliqua indecentia cum iniuria tanti Sacramenti timeri potest."

[10] *Rituale Romanum*, tit. IV, cap. 4, *communione infirmorum*, n. 2: "Sanctum Viaticum infirmis ne nimium differatur; et qui animarum curam gerunt, sedulo advigilent ut eo infirmi plene sui compotes reficiantur."

[11] Canon 858, § 1. Qui a media nocte ieiunium naturale non servaverit, nequit ad sanctissimam Eucharistiam admitti, nisi mortis urgeat periculum, aut necessitas impediendi irreverentiam in sacramentum.

sequently, after an unconsecrated particle has been administered and it is still uncertain that no danger of irreverence is present, Viaticum should not be administered.

The presence of a persistent cough may or may not constitute a danger of irreverence to the Sacred Species. If the cough is so severe that as a result the patient is unable to swallow, then, obviously, no attempt to administer Viaticum should be made. But if the sick person is capable of swallowing the Host, or a small fraction thereof, Viaticum may be given. No danger of irreverence need be feared from the fact that the patient constantly expectorates phlegm. Phlegm which comes to the mouth as a result of severe coughing has its origin in the trachea, or the passage which leads to the lungs, and not in the esophagus, or the passage which leads to the stomach. If a sick person can swallow the Host securely, then there is no danger that he will cough It up.[12]

Vomiting is another potential cause of irreverence which may prohibit the reception of Viaticum. It may result from the taking of food, or it may occur independently of eating or drinking. In the first case the use of an unconsecrated particle in order to test the patient's ability to retain the Host long enough for digestion is a satisfactory practical procedure. If, after the unconsecrated particle is swallowed, vomiting does not occur for half an hour, the minister of Viaticum can be reasonably certain that no danger of irreverence is to be feared, and can then proceed to administer the Sacrament.[13]

Noldin required freedom from vomiting for an hour after the reception of an unconsecrated particle before allowing the administration of Viaticum.[14] This requirement seems unduly strict in view of the fact that twenty minutes or half an hour is sufficient time for the digestion of the Host. Consequently the writer prefers the viewpoint of O'Kane-Fallon and Regatilo, who require freedom from vomiting for only half an hour before allowing the minister

[12] Cf. Liguori, *Theologia Moralis,* Lib. VI, *de Eucharistia,* n. 292; Regatillo, *Ius Sacramentarium,* I, 179; O'Kane-Fallon, *Notes on the Rubrics of the Roman Ritual,* p. 400.

[13] Cf. O'Kane-Fallon, *loc. cit.;* Regatillo, *loc. cit.*

[14] *Summa Theologiae Moralis,* III, p. 154, n. 139.

to communicate the sick person. Viaticum should not be given to one who vomits independently of whether he has or has not taken food, unless he has been free from vomiting for at least six hours.[15]

The practice of allowing children who have reached the use of reason to die without receiving Viaticum has been condemned as an utterly detestable abuse, and local ordinaries have been instructed to proceed severely against those who do not abandon the practice.[16] Children who enjoy the qualifications specified in canon 854, § 2, have a strict right to receive Viaticum, and accordingly pastors are bound in virtue of their office to administer It to them.[17]

The decree *Quam singulari* made no distinction between the dispositions required for the reception of Viaticum and the dispositions required for the reception of simple Holy Communion. The legislation contained in canon 854, § 3, which specifies the dispositions necessary for simple Holy Communion, is substantially the same as that contained in n. III of the cited decree.[18] Considerably less intellectual preparation for the reception of Viaticum is demanded by the Code.[19] Consequently children may now be more readily allowed to receive Viaticum than to receive simple Holy Communion.

It is scarcely necessary for the writer to discuss again in detail the dispositions necessary for the reception of Viaticum. It suffices

[15] Liguori, *loc. cit.;* Regatillo, *loc. cit.*

[16] S. C. de Sacr., decr. 8 aug. 1910, n. VIII: "Detestabilis omnino est abusus non ministrandi Viaticum es Extremum Unctionem pueris post usum rationis eosque sepeliendi ritu parvulorum. In eos, qui ab huiusmodi more non recedant, Ordinarii locorum severe animadvertant."—*AAS,* II (1910), 583; *Fontes,* n. 2103.

[17] Canon 467, § 1. Debet parochus officia divina celebrare, administrare sacramenta fidelibus, quoties legitime petant, . . .

[18] "Cognitio religionis quae in puero, ut ipse ad primam Communionem convenienter se praeparet, ea est, qua ipse fidei mysteria necessaria necessitate medii pro suo captu percipiat, atque eucharisticum panem a communi et corporali distinguat ut ea devotione quam ipsius fert aetas ad SS. Eucharistiam accedat."—*AAS,* II (1910), 582; *Fontes,* n. 2103.

[19] Canon 854, § 2. In periculo mortis, ut sanctissima Eucharistia pueris ministrari possit ac debeat, satis est ut sciant Corpus Christi a communi cibo discernere illudque reventer adorare.

to note briefly, in passing, the difference between the requirements for the reception of simple Holy Communion on the one hand, and for the reception of Viaticum on the other hand.

It may be stated as a general rule that the conditions necessary for the fruitful reception of Viaticum are less exacting than those required for the reception of simple Holy Communion. The requisite state of grace demanded in all communicants alike is of course a point regarding which no difference obtains under any given circumstances. The Eucharist can never be fruitfully received by one who is in the state of mortal sin. Such a person can still receive Holy Communion sacramentally, but at the same time he receives It unfruitfully.[20]

Outside the danger of death an explicit intention of receiving the Eucharist is demanded, but an implicit intention suffices when the danger of death is present.[21]

No great degree of devotion can be expected of children who receive first Holy Communion by way of Viaticum. The greater their knowledge of the Blessed Sacrament, the greater also the degree of devotion expected from them.[22]

Children who receive first Holy Communion by way of Viaticum are not required to have a knowledge of the mysteries of faith absolutely necessary for salvation. It suffices if they can distinguish the Body of Christ from common bread.[23] Likewise the recipients of Viaticum are not required to observe the law of the natural fast.[24] Neither uncleanliness of person, nor squalor of dress, nor wretchedness of living conditions, stands in the way of the reception of Viaticum.[25]

Occasionally a doubt may arise as to whether a child enjoys the requisite qualifications for admission to Viaticum. The min-

[20] Conc. Trident., sess. XIII, *de Eucharistia,* c. 8—Schroeder, *Canons and Decrees of the Council of Trent,* p. 354.

[21] Cf. *supra,* p. 60.

[22] Conc. Trident., sess. XIII, *de Eucharistia,* c. 7—Schroeder, *loc. cit.*

[23] Canon 854, § 2.

[24] Canon 858, § 1.

[25] Cf. Alexander VII, const. *Sacrosancti,* 18 iam. 1658, § 2, n. 13: "Aegrotis morti proximis cuiuscumque sint conditionis, quamvis in sordido, ac vili degant loco, aut tugurio, Sacrum Eucharistiae Viaticum deferatur, . . ."—*Fontes,* n. 235.

ister of Viaticum may be uncertain whether a child in danger of death has acquired a sufficient use of reason or possesses the dispositions mentioned in the preceding paragraph. What are his obligations when such a doubt arises?

Canonists teach that there is no strict obligation to administer Viaticum when there is uncertainty as to whether a child has attained the years of discretion. The teaching of Coronata on this point is not clear. On the one hand he states that, when such a doubt arises, the child's completion of the seventh year should be the deciding factor in the admission of it to, or the refusal to it of, Viaticum. If the child has completed its seventh year, Viaticum should be given; if it has not completed its seventh year, the Sacrament should not be administered.[26] On the other hand he seems to depart from this rule when he teaches that, when there is question of administering Viaticum and there is present a doubt as to the child's capacity, the obligation to receive does not bind, but that nevertheless the Sacrament may be administered.[27]

The best solution for the problem is the one commonly advocated by canonists, namely, that in such circumstances there is no strict obligation to administer Viaticum, though the minister is free to do so. They state it as the more laudable practice to administer Viaticum to such a child, since under the circumstances there is question of a law which is favorable to the child—*"favores convenit ampliari."*[28] In view of the severe penalties which may be inflicted on a minister who dares to administer the sacraments to those to whom their reception is prohibited by divine or by ecclesiastical law, it is unreasonable to oblige him to administer Viaticum to a

[26] "Atque iuxta supradictam praesumptionem solvenda erit quaestio quam proponebant theologi: an dandum sit Viaticum quando dubitatur de pueri capacitate; seu in dubio dandum est, septennio expleto, negandum ante septennium."—*Tractatus Canonicus de Sacramentis,* I, 289.

[27] "In dubio utrum puer in periculo mortis usum rationis habeat obligatio non urget, at potest Viaticum ministrari."—*Op. cit.,* I, 321.

[28] Cf. McNicholas, "The Age of Children for First Communion"—*AER,* XLIII (1910), 487; Noldin-Schmitt, *Summa Theologia Moralis,* III, 143; Cappello, *De Sacramentis,* I, 399; O'Kane-Fallon, *Notes on the Rubrics of the Roman Ritual,* p. 319.

child when he doubts whether he may lawfully do so.[29] At the same time the spirit of the legislation contained in the Code seems to indicate that Viaticum should be administered in such circumstances. Consequently the writer favors the opinion of canonists who teach that the minister of Viaticum may, but has no strict obligation to, administer Viaticum when he doubts whether the subject has attained the years of discretion. He need have no scruples about resolving his doubts in favor of communicating the child.

When it is doubted whether a child which is in danger of death has a sufficient knowledge for the reception of Viaticum the duty of the pastor is clear. Canon 1330, 2°, enjoins on the pastor the strict obligation of preparing children for admission to first Holy Communion.[30] This obligation of instruction applies equally to children who make their first Holy Communion in the ordinary way and to children who receive It as Viaticum. Should the pastor be called upon to attend a child when it is in danger of death, and should he then discover that, even though the child has reached the use of reason, it has no concept of what the Eucharist is, he is bound there and then to give the necessary instruction. Quasi-pastors, parochial administrators, parochial substitute vicars, parochial adjutant priests and parochial assistant priests would have a like obligation in similar circumstances.[31]

The obligation of the above mentioned priests is an obligation arising from justice: another priest or a deacon,[32] if called for some

[29] Canon 2364. Minister qui ausus fuerit Sacramenta administrare illis qui iure sive divino sive ecclesiastico eadem recipere prohibentur, suspendatur ab administrandis Sacramentis per tempus prudenti Ordinarii arbitrio definiendum aliisque poenis pro gravitate culpae puniatur, firmis peculiaribus poenis in aliqua huius generis delicta iure statutis.

The penalties mentioned in this canon are of a *ferendae sententiae* character—Cf. Chelodi, *De Delictis et Poenis*, p. 133.

[30] Canon 1330, 2°. Debet parochus: Peculiari omnino studio, praesertim, si nihil obsit, Quadragesimae tempore, pueros sic instituere ut sancte Sancta primum de altari libent.

[31] Cf. *supra*, pp. 113-114.

[32] According to canon 845, § 2, a deacon is the extraordinary minister of Holy Communion. He may act as minister with the permission of the ordinary or of the pastor, and may presume this permission in any case of necessity.

legitimate reason to attend the child, would be bound in charity to administer Viaticum and, if necessary, to dispose the child for Its reception.[33]

It is impossible to state how long a time should be employed for the imparting of the necessary instruction. To a great extent its duration will depend on the mental capacity of the child, as also on its moral disposition. In any case it is necessary that the child know that Christ, the Son of God, became Man, and that He is really, truly and substantially present in the Blessed Eucharist. In case the minister has remained in doubt regarding the sufficiency of the child's knowledge, and if time does not permit any further instruction, either because death is approaching or because the subject is becoming unconscious, the minister may resolve his doubt in favor of admitting the child to Viaticum for the same reason which allows him to administer this Sacrament when there exists a doubt as to whether the child has attained the use of reason.

[33] Cf. Cappello, *De Sacramentis,* I, 343.

CHAPTER VIII

FIRST COMMUNION DAY

IN many parishes it is customary to assemble all the children of the first Communion class in order to admit them to Holy Communion in a body. The children are expected to attend a certain Mass, to occupy reserved pews, and then to approach the altar in processional order. Consideration is given in this chapter as to whether this custom is in full accord with the spirit of the law, or whether it is more desirable to admit children individually, that is, without obliging them to receive first Holy Communion in a group.

In France during the nineteenth century the reception of first Holy Communion was an occasion of considerable solemnity. The splendor of the ceremony which accompanied the admission of the young communicants was calculated to edify the spectators and to make the younger children long for the day when they too would be allowed to approach the altar for the first time. A rather advanced age and a continued attendance at catechism classes for a certain number of years were demanded as necessary conditions for inclusion among those who were about to receive first Holy Communion.[1] It was thought that this practice would achieve much good by inducing children to receive a solid grounding in Catholic doctrine. Too frequently the results were deplorable. By the time the children were allowed to receive the Eucharist they had lost their pristine innocence: unable to obtain the spiritual nourishment they so needed, they had succumbed to temptation.[2]

[1] E. g., in 1884 the Bishop of Annecy in a pastoral letter ruled that the completion of the twelfth year and a continued attendance at catechism classes for the two preceding years were essential conditions for admission to the reception of first Communion.—Cf. *Thesaurus*, CXLVII (1888), 474-487; *Le Canoniste Contemporain*, XII (1889), 154.

[2] S. C. de Sacr. decr. 8 aug. 1910: "Etiamsi vero primae Communioni diligentior institutio et accurata sacramentalis Confessio praemittatur, quod quidem non ubique fit, dolenda tamen semper est primae innocentiae iactura, quae, sumpta tenerioribus annis Eucharistia, poterat fortasse vitari."—*AAS*, II (1910), 579; *Fontes*, n. 2103.

Because of the evil results accruing from the custom, the Sacred Congregation of the Sacraments, in the decree *Quam singulari*, commanded that children be privately admitted to Holy Communion when they had reached the age of discretion. The decree sanctioned the holding of a general Communion of children at least once a year, and directed that those who had already made their first Communion should likewise take part in it.[3]

No mention of the holding of a general Communion is found in the Code. This omission is significant in view of the fact that the remaining norms of the decree *Quam singulari* are embodied in the canons of the Code.[4] The silence of the legislator regarding any general Communion of children must be interpreted as meaning that the idea of such a Communion was falling into disfavor, or that at least it was no longer recommended.[5]

On December 8, 1938, the Sacred Congregation of the Sacraments issued a reserved Instruction dealing with daily Communion and with the precautions to be taken against possible attending abuses. Even though the Instruction does not deal explicitly with the correction of abuses possible in the reception of first Holy Communion, some of its norms may be used with a view to determining whether the custom of admitting children to first Communion in groups is the ideal method of admission.

The object of the Instruction is to prescribe remedies for the

[3] N. V—*AAS*, II (1910), 582; *Fontes*, n. 2103.

[4] Compare N. I of *Quam singulari* with canon 88, § 3, and 860;
Compare N. II of *Quam singulari* with canon 1331;
Compare N. III of *Quam singulari* with canon 854, § 3;
Compare N. IV of *Quam singulari* with canon 854, § 4, and 860;
Compare N. V of *Quam singulari* with canon 863;
Compare N. VII of *Quam singulari* with canon 906;
Compare N. VIII of *Quam singulari* with canon 854, § 2, and 864, § 1.
For the text of the cited sections of *Quam singulari* cf. *AAS*, II (1910), 582-583; *Fontes*, n. 2103.

[5] The writer does not mean to imply that he regards admission to Holy Communion in classes as being the equivalent of the "general Communion" spoken of in the decree *Quam singulari*. His object in bringing up the question of a general Communion is to show that the norms which regulate the holding of such a Communion are applicable also to the question of group admission to first Holy Communion.

prevention of unworthy Communion. Lest it be thought that the writer is beating the air in discussing the possibility of an unworthy first Communion, it is in order to point out again that the contention of the theologians [6] who maintain that a greater use of reason is required for the commission of mortal sin than for the commission of venial sin is by no means certain. In point of fact the teaching that the ability to commit venial sin connotes the ability to commit mortal sin seems to be the doctrine favored by the Church. St. Thomas, the teaching of whose doctrine is obligatory in seminaries,[7] asserted that that use of reason which suffices for the commission of venial sin suffices also for the commission of mortal sin.[8]

The decree *Quam singulari* reprobated the custom of not allowing children who had reached the age of discretion to seek sacramental absolution. The motivating cause for this reprobation was the fact that, if such children were unfortunate enough to fall into *mortal* sin, they could not regain the state of grace through sacramental confession for a long time.[9] In view of the teaching of St. Thomas and of the statements of the decree *Quam singulari*, it is obvious that an application of the norms of the Instruction of the Sacred Congregation to the method of admitting children to first Holy Communion is quite practicable and even necessary.

In communities of boys and girls there should never be an announcement of a *general Communion* with special solemnity. Outside such communities the name "general Communion" should either not be used at all or, if it be used, its meaning should be care-

[6] E. g., Coronata, *Tractatus Canonicus de Sacramentis*, I, 291.

[7] Canon 1366, § 2.

[8] *Summa Theologica*, I-II, q. 89, art. 6: "Impossibile est quod peccatum veniale sit in aliquo cum originali peccato absque mortali . . . Cum usus rationis habere inceperit, non omnino excusatur a culpa venialis et mortalis peccati."

[9] "Nec minus est reprobandus mos pluribus vigens in locis, quo sacramentalis Confessio inhibetur pueris nondum ad eucharisticam mensam admissis, aut iisdem absolutio non impertitur. Quo fit ut ipsi *peccatorum fortasse gravium* laqueis irretiti magno cum periculo diu iaceant. . . .
N. VII: Consuetudo non admittendi ad confessionem pueros, aut nunquam eos absolvendi, *quum ad usum rationis pervenerint*, est omnino improbanda. . . ."—*AAS*, II (1910), 579-583; *Fontes*, n. 2103. (Italics inserted by the writer).

fully explained, namely, that all are invited to the Holy Table, but that no one is obliged to approach, and that, on the contrary, each individual is entirely free to forego the invitation.[10]

The spirit of this norm may be easily violated through the practice of admitting together a whole class of children to first Holy Communion. There is present a danger that a child may approach the altar with an unquiet conscience, since it believes that it is obliged along with the others to receive Holy Communion. It may not be so easy to convince children of their freedom to abstain from approaching the Holy Table. Children are usually very sensitive to the opinion of their companions. They realize that abstinence from Holy Communion on the appointed day may result in curious inquiries and hurtful remarks. Hence there is a danger that a child may go forward to receive Holy Communion with its companions, even though it is conscious of being in the state of mortal sin, in order to avoid compromising its good name.

A further relevant norm of the Instruction urges that, when Holy Communion is being received, all those things are to be avoided which create greater difficulty for a young person who wishes to abstain from Holy Communion. Arrangements must be such that his abstinence will not be noticed. Hence there should be no express invitation, no rigid and quasi-military order in coming up, no insignia to be worn by those who receive Holy Communion, etc.[11]

This norm brings to notice another undesirable feature of group admission to first Holy Communion. In many places where such a custom is in vogue it is usual to have the young communicants kneel together in reserved pews near the altar rail. When the time to receive the Eucharist approaches, they are required to walk to the altar rail in processional order, the result being that if a particular child remains in its place it is left in conspicuous isolation. There is no necessity to labor the point that this is precisely the situation which the cited norm of the Instruction aims at preventing.

Another disadvantage of group admission to first Holy Communion is the fact that such a method of admission may furnish an

[10] *Reserved Instruction* of the Sacred Congregation of the Sacraments, December 8, 1938, n. II, 3 (b)—Bouscaren, *The Canon Law Digest,* II, 213.

[11] N. III, 3 (c)—Bouscaren, *op. cit.,* II, 214.

occasion for a child to approach the altar without the proper intention. A child may go to Holy Communion merely in imitation of its companions and without the intention of gaining an increase of grace. Or it may receive the Eucharist along with its companions merely to please its parents, knowing that they will be disappointed if it fails to receive along with its classmates. Neither of these intentions constitutes a proper intention for the reception of Holy Communion.[12]

All things considered, it is more in keeping with the spirit of the Instruction of the Sacred Congregation of the Sacraments not to admit children to first Holy Communion in classes or groups. Some of the disadvantages of such a practice have been considered. Its advantages are negligible. The spectacle of a number of innocents marching together to receive Our Lord for the first time may possibly be a source of edification for the spectators. One must not, however, confuse edification with the mere arousing of interest. Many of the congregation see in the ceremony nothing more than an unusual parade. It is likewise doubtful if the children themselves derive any spiritual benefit from the ceremony. The care they must exercise in observing processional order in going to and from the altar rail is a fertile source of distraction for young minds.

On the other hand, none of these disadvantages derive from the individual admission of children to the reception of the Eucharist. Freedom of conscience is safeguarded by the fact that each child is allowed to choose any morning it wishes on which to approach the altar. There can be no occasion for hurtful remarks by its companions if it fails to receive on any particular morning. There is present no regimentation with its attendant distractions to disturb the child in its preparation and thanksgiving. In other words, the child is at liberty to make its first Holy Communion when it feels that it can do so with the greatest spiritual benefit.

Whatever method of admission be followed, those whose duty

[12] S. C. C. decr. *"Sacra Tridentina Synodus,"* 20 dec. 1905: "Recta autem mens in eo est, ut qui ad sacram Mensam accedit, non usui aut vanitati aut humanis rationibus indulgeat, sed Dei placito satisfacere velit, ei arctius caritate coniungi, ac divino illo pharmaco suis infirmitatibus ac defectibus occurrere."—*Fontes,* n. 2103.

it is to prepare children for Holy Communion should emphasize the fact that a child is not obliged in any way to present itself at the altar on a determined morning. They should convince their charges that abstinence from Holy Communion on any occasion does not involve any stigma, but evinces rather a sign of a tender and delicate conscience. The ultimate end of the course of preparation is not that children who attend it merely present themselves at the altar rail, but that they receive the Eucharist piously.[18]

[18] Canon 1330, 2°. Debet parochus: Peculiari omnino studio, praesertim, si nihil obsit, Quadragesimae tempore, pueros sic instituere ut *sancte* Sancta primum de altari libent. (Italics inserted by the writer).

CONCLUSIONS

As a result of this study the following conclusions are offered:

1. The possession of the qualifications enumerated in canon 854, §§ 2-3, is a test which at once indicates the enjoyment of sufficient discretion and instruction for the reception of first Holy Communion.

2. Children are not bound to receive Holy Communion immediately after attaining the years of discretion. They are, however, obliged to approach the altar during the following Paschal season, even though they have not yet completed their seventh year.

3. The word *"gustus,"* as found in canon 854, § 1, should be interpreted as meaning "intellectual appreciation."

4. Compliance with the spirit of the law demands that children should be prepared for, and admitted to, first Holy Communion immediately after attaining the years of discretion.

5. The prerogative of admitting children to first Holy Communion is simply the competence to implement the judgment of their possession of the requisite dispositions. The confessor and the parents enjoy equal but not exclusive competence in this matter. The pastor can, for a legitimate reason, question the decision of either. In practice, however, he should never interfere with the decision of the confessor. In case he questions the decision of the parents his judgment must be honored when the dispute centers on the sufficiency of the child's intellectual qualifications: the decision of the parents prevails when the child's possession of a sufficient use of reason is challenged.

6. Individual admission to first Holy Communion is to be preferred to group admission. Group admission can be tolerated only if the children are free to abstain from approaching the altar, should they so desire, without any embarrassment.

BIBLIOGRAPHY

Sources

Acta Apostolicae Sedis, Commentarium Officiale, Romae, 1909-1929; Civitate Vaticana, 1929—.

Acta et Decreta Concilii Plenarii Americae Latinae in Urbe Celebrati, Romae: Typis Vaticanis, 1900.

Acta et Decreta Concilii Plenarii Australasiae Habiti apud Sydney A.D. 1885, a sancta Sede Recognita, Sydney: Cunningham, 1887.

Acta et Decreta Concilii Plenarii Baltimorensis Tertii, Baltimore: John Murphy, 1886.

Acta et Decreta Concilii Provincialis Portlandensis in Oregon Quarti anno MCMXXXII, Portland: Sentinel Printery, 1932.

Acta et Decreta Sacrorum Conciliorum Recentiorum, Collectio Lacensis, Auctoribus Presbyteris S. J. e domo B. V. M. sine Labe Conceptae ad Lacum, 7 vols., Friburgi Brisgoviae, 1870-1890.

Acta et Statuta Synodi Richmondiensis Secundae, Baltimore: John Murphy, 1886.

Bruns, H. T., *Canones Apostolorum et Conciliorum saeculorum IV-VII,* 2 vols., Berolini: Reimeri, 1839.

Catechetical Documents of Pope Pius X, translated and edited by Joseph B. Collins, Paterson: St. Anthony Guild Press, 1946.

Catechismus ex decreto Concilii Tidentini ad parochos Pii V Pontificis Max. et deinde Clementis XIII. iussu editus ed. stereotypa, Taurini-Romae: Marietti, 1930.

Codex Iuris Canonici Pii X Pontificis Maximi iussu digestus Benedicti XV auctoritate promulgatus, Romae: Typis Polyglottis Vaticanis, 1917.

Codicis Iuris Canonici Fontes, cura Emi Card. Gasparri editi, 9 vols., Romae-Civitate Vaticana: Typis Polyglottis Vaticanis, 1923-1939. (Vols. VII-IX, ed. cura et studio Emi Iustiniani Card. Seredi).

Collectanea S. Congregationis de Propaganda Fide, 2 vols., Romae: Typographia Polyglotta S. C. de Propaganda Fide, 1907.

Decretales D. Gregorii Papae IX, una cum Glossis restitutae, Romae, 1582.

Denziger, H.-Bannwart, C.-Umberg, J. B., *Enchiridion Symbolorum, Definitionum, et Declarationum de Rebus Fidei et Morum,* 21.-23. ed., Friburgi Brisgoviae: Herder, 1937.

Griffith, Paul, *The Priest's New Ritual,* Baltimore: John Murphy, 1940.

Hardouin, Jean, *Acta Conciliorum et Epistolae Decretales ac Constitutiones Summorum Pontificum,* 12 vols., Parisiis 1714-1715.

Mansi, J. D., *Sacrorum Conciliorum Nova et Amplissima Collectio,* 53 vols. in 60, Paris-Leipzig-Arnhem, 1901-1927.

Rituale Romanum Pauli V Pontificis Maximi iussu editum aliorumque Pontificum cura recognitum atque auctoritate Pii Papae XI ad normam Codicis Iuris Canonici accommodatum, 2. ed. iuxta Typicam Vaticanam amplificata I, New York: Benziger, 1925.

Rituale Romanum, Pauli V Maxima iussu editum, et a Benedicto XIV Auctum et Castigatum, Baltimore: John Murphy, 1873.

Schroeder, H. J., *Canons and Decrees of the Council of Trent*, St. Louis: Herder, 1941.

Synodus Dioecesana Petriunculana Prima, Petriunculae: apud Cancellariam Dioecesanam, 1909.

Thesaurus Resolutionum Sacrae Congregationis Concilii, 167 vols., Romae, 1718-1908.

REFERENCE WORKS

Aertnys, J.-Damen, C. A., *Theologia Moralis*, 13. ed., 2 vols., Taurini-Romae: Marietti, 1939.

Anglin, Thomas F., *The Eucharistic Fast*, The Catholic University of America Canon Law Studies, no. 124, Washington, D. C.: The Catholic University of America Press, 1941.

Aquinas, St. Thomas, *Opera Omnia, studio et labore Stanislai Edwardi Frette et Pauli Mare*, 34 vols., Vol. X, Parisiis: Vivès, 1837.

———, *Summa Theologica*, 12. ed., 6 vols., Taurini: Marietti, 1937-1938.

Augustine, Charles, *A Commentary on Canon Law*, 8 vols., Vol. IV, 3. ed., St. Louis: Herder, 1925.

Ayrinhac, H. A., *Legislation on the Sacraments*, New York: Longmans, Green and Co., 1928.

Benedictus XIV, *De Synodo Dioecesana*, 4 vols., Mechliniae, 1842.

———, *Opera Omnia*, 17 vols., Vol. XIV, Prati: Ghettus et Soc., 1846.

Berutti, Christophorus, *Institutiones Iuris Canonici*, 6 vols., Vol. I, Taurini-Romae: Marietti, 1936.

Beste, Udalricus, *Introductio in Codicem*, ed. altera, Collegeville: St. John's Abbey Press, 1944.

Blat, Albertus, *Commentarium Textus Codicis Iuris Canonici*, 5 vols. in 6, Vol. III, Pars I (*De Sacramentis*), Romae: Ex Typographia Pontificia Pii X, 1920.

Borromaeus, St. Carolus, *Pastorum Instructiones*, Gandae: Van der Schelden, 1828.

Bouscaren, T. Lincoln, *The Canon Law Digest*, 2 vols., Milwaukee: Bruce Publishing Company, 1934-1943.

Cappello, Felix M., *De aetate admittendorum ad primam Communionem Eucharisticam*, Romae: Typis Cuggiani, 1911.

———, *Summa Iuris Canonici*, 3 vols., Vol. II, 3. ed., Romae: Apud aedes Universitatis Gregorianae, 1939.

———, *Tractatus Canonico-Moralis de Sacramentis,* 3 vols. in 6, Vol. I, 4. ed., Romae: Marietti, 1945.

Castropalao, Ferdinandus, *Opera Omnia,* 7 vols., Lugduni: Barbier, 1682.

Chelodi, Ioannes, *Ius Canonicum de Delictis et Poenis,* 5. ed., Vicenza: Societa' Anonima Tipografica, 1943.

Cicognani, Amleto Giovanni, *Canon Law,* Philadelphia: Dolphin Press, 1934.

Cigno, Giustino, *Giovanni Andrea Serrao e il Giansenismo nell' Italia Meridionale,* Palermo, Scuola Tipografica R. Istituto d'Assistenzo, 1938.

Clinton, Connell, *The Paschal Precept,* The Catholic University of America Canon Law Studies, no. 73, Washington, D. C.: The Catholic University of America, 1932.

Cocchi, Guidus, *Commentarium in Codicem Iuris Canonici,* 8 vols. in 5, Vol. VI, 3. ed., 1933, Vol. VII, 3. ed., 1940, Taurinorum Augustae: Marietti.

Corblet, Jules, *Histoire Dogmatique, Liturgique et Archéologique de Sacrement de L'Eucharistie,* 2 vols., Paris: Societé Générale de Librairie Catholique, 1885.

Coronata, Mattheus Conte a, *Institutiones Iuris Canonici ad Usum Utriusque Cleri et Scholarum,* 5 vols., Vols. I-IV, 2. ed., 1939-1945, Vol. V, 1936, Taurini: Marietti.

———, *Tractatus Canonicus de Sacramentis,* 3 vols., Romae: Marietti, 1943-1945.

D'Annibale, Josephus, *Summula Theologiae Moralis,* 4. ed., 3 vols., Romae: Ex Typographia Polyglotta, 1894.

Davis, Henry, *Moral and Pastoral Theology,* 4. ed., 4 vols., New York: Sheed and Ward, 1943.

De Lugo, Ioannes, *Disputationes Scholasticae et Morales,* ed. nova, 8 vols., Parisiis: Vivès, 1868-1869.

De Meester, A., *Juris Canonici et Juris Canonico-Civilis Compendium,* ed. nova, 3 vols. in 4, Brugis: Descleé, 1921-1928.

De Smet, A., *Tractatus Dogmatico-Moralis de Sacramentis in Genere,* ed., altera, Brugis: Beyaert, 1924.

Doheny, William J., *Canonical Procedure in Matrimonial Cases,* 2 vols., Vol. II, Milwaukee: The Bruce Publishing Company, 1944.

Duchesne, Louis, *Christian Worship, its origin and evolution:* translated from the third French edition by M. L. McClure, London: Society for Promoting Christian Knowledge, 1903.

Durieux, P.-Dolphin, O., *The Eucharist, Law and Practice,* Chicago, The Lakeside Press, 1926.

Evagrius, *A History of the Church in six books from A.D. 431 to A.D. 594.* A New Translation from the Greek, London: Samuel Bagster and Sons, 1846.

Fanfani, Ludovicus, *De Iure Parochorum,* Taurini-Romae: Marietti, 1924.

Ferreres, Ioannes, *Institutiones Canonicae,* 2 vols., Vol. II, ed. altera, Barcinone: Ex Typis Eugenii Subirana, 1920.

Ferreres, Juan B., *The Decree on Daily Communion*, English translation by H. Jimenez, St. Louis: Herder, 1909.

Gasparri, Petrus, *Tractatus Canonicus de Sanctissima Eucharistia*, 2 vols., Parisiis: Delhomme et Briguet, 1897.

Genicot, Eduardus, *Theologicae Moralis Institutiones*, 6. ed., 2 vols., Bruxellis: Dewit, 1909.

Gury, J. P.-Ballerini, A., *Compendium Theologiae Moralis*, 9. ed., 2 vols., Romae: Ex Typographia Polyglotta, 1887.

Kenrick, Francis P., *Theologia Moralis*, 3 vols., Mechliniae: Dessain, 1861.

Lehmkuhl, Augustinus, *Theologia Moralis*, 4. ed., 2 vols., Friburgi-Brisgoviae: Herder, 1887.

Liguori, St. Alphonsus, *Theologiae Moralis*, 4 vols., Taurini: Marietti, 1872.

Mabillon, Jean, *Musaeum Italicum*, 2 vols., Parisiis: Montelant, 1724.

Maringola, Aloisius, *Antiquitatum Christianarum Institutiones*, 2. ed., 2 vols., Neapoli: Pelella, 1862.

Martène, Edmundus, *De Antiquis Ecclesiae Ritibus*, 4 vols., Rotomagi: Sumptibus Guillelmi Behourt, 1700.

McCloskey, Joseph A., *The Subject of Ecclesiastical Law according to Canon 12*, The Catholic University of America Canon Law Studies, no. 165, Washington, D. C.: The Catholic University of America Press, 1942.

Merkelbach, Benedictus H., *Summa Theologiae Moralis*, 3. ed., 3 vols., Desclée, 1939.

Michiels, Gommarus, *Normae Generales Iuris Canonici*, 2 vols., Lublin: Universitas Catholica, 1929.

Migne, P. J., *Patrologiae Cursus Completus, Series Graeca*, 161 vols., Parisiis, 1856-1866.

———, *Patrologiae Cursus Completus, Series Latina*, 221 vols., Parisiis, 1844-1864.

Munn, Norman L., *Psychological Development*, Cambridge: Riverside Press, 1938.

Muratori, Ludovicus A., *Liturgia Romana Vetus*, 2 vols., Neapoli: Typis Cajetani Castellani, 1776.

Noldin, H., *Summa Theologiae Moralis*, 5. ed., 3 vols., Oeniponte: F. Rauch, 1904.

Noldin, H.-Schmitt, A., *Summa Theologiae Moralis iuxta Codicem Iuris Canonici*, 3 vols., Vols. I, III, 23. ed., 1935, Vol. II, 22. ed., 1934, Oeniponte: Typis et Sumptibus Fel. Rauch.

Noval, J., *Commentarium Codicis Iuris Canonici, Lib. IV, De Processibus*, 2 vols., Romae, 1920-1932.

Ojetti, B. *Commentarium in Codicem Iuris Canonici*, 4 vols., Romae: Universitas Gregoriana, 1927-1931.

O'Kane, J.-Fallon, M. J., *Notes on the Rubrics of the Roman Ritual*, 4. ed., Dublin: Duffy, 1938.

Oppenheim, Philippus, *Institutiones systematico-historicae in Sacram Liturgiam, Pars II, Liturgia specialis,* Series II, *Liturgia Sacramentalis (Ritualis et Pontificalis),* Vol. I, *De fontibus et historia ritus baptismalis,* Taurini-Romae: Marietti, 1943.

Payen, G., *De Matrimonio in Missionibus,* 3 vols., Vol. II, ed. altera, Zi-ka-wei: In typographia T'ou-se-we, 1936.

Petavius, Dionysius, *Dogmata Theologica,* 8 vols., ed. nova, Parisiis: Vives, 1866-1868.

Pohle, J.-Preuss, A., *The Sacraments,* 4 vols., 3. ed., St. Louis: Herder, 1919-1920.

Prümmer, Dom. M., *Manuale Theologiae Moralis,* 3 vols., Vol. I, 8. ed., Vol. II, 4 et 5. ed., Vol. III, 6. et 7. ed., Friburgi-Brisgoviae: Herder, 1928-1935.

Rapin, René de, *Memoirs,* 2 vols., Paris: Gaume Freres et J. Duprey, 1865.

Regatillo, Eduardus F., *Ius Sacramentarium,* 2 vols., Santander: Sal Terrae, 1945-1946.

Sabetti, A.-Barrett, T., *Compendium Theologiae Moralis,* 27. ed., New York: Pustet, 1919.

Sartori, P. C., *Enchiridion Canonicum,* 6. ed., Vicetiae: Ex Typographia Commerciali, 1938.

Schroeder, H. J., *Disciplinary Decrees of the General Councils,* St. Louis: Herder, 1937.

Schulze, Frederick, *A Manual of Pastoral Theology,* 3. ed., London: Herder, 1939. (Reprint of 3. ed., 1923.)

Sipos, Stephanus, *Enchiridion Iuris Canonici,* Pécs: Ex Typographis "Haladás R. T.," 1926.

Suarez, Franciscus, *Opera Omnia,* ed. nova, 28 vols., Parisiis: Vivès, 1856-1866.

Tanquerey, Ad., *Synopsis Theologiae Dogmaticae,* 22. ed., 3 vols., Parisiis: Desclée, 1930.

———, *Synopsis Theologiae Moralis et Pastoralis,* 7. ed., 3 vols., Romae: Desclée, 1920.

Telch, Carolus, *Epitome Theologiae Moralis,* 6. ed., Oeniponte: Rauch, 1924.

Van Hove, A., *De Legibus Ecclesiasticis,* Mechliniae-Romae: Dessain, 1930.

Vasquez, Gabrielis, *Libri Commentariorum in Tertiam Partem S. Thomae,* 9 vols., Lugduni: Sumptibus Jacobi Cardon, 1630-1631.

Vermeersch, A., *Theologia Moralis,* 2. ed., 4 vols., Romae: Università Gregoriana, 1926-1928.

Vermeersch, A.-Creusen, I., *Epitome Iuris Canonici,* 3 vols., Vol. II, 4. ed., Mechliniae-Romae, 1930.

Wernz, F.-Vidal, P., *Ius Canonicum ad Codicis Normam Exactum,* 7 tomes in 8 vols., Vol. IV, Pars 2, 1935, Vol. VI, 1927, Romae: Apud Aedes Universitatis Gregorianae.

Wilson, H. A., *The Gelasian Sacramentary,* Oxford: The Clarendon Press, 1894.

Woywod, Stanislaus, *A Practical Commentary on the Code of Canon Law,* 9. ed., 2 vols., New York: Wagner, 1945.

Articles

Anonymous, "Questions des Sciences Ecclésiastiques"—*L'Ami du Clergé.* XLVI (1929), 88-89.

Gillmann, Franz, "Die *'anni discretionis'* im Kanon *'Omnis utriusque Sexus'* "—*AKKR,* CVIII (1928), 556-617.

McNicholas, J. T., "The Age of Children for First Communion"—*AER,* XLIII (1910), 485.

Murphy, Francis J., "General Norms of Canon Law as found in the First Book of the Code"—*The Jurist,* IV (1944), 386.

O'Donnell, M. J., "The Admission of Children to Holy Communion"—*IER,* 5. series, III (1914), 82.

———, "The Decree *'Quam singulari'*—Has the Parish Priest, as such, the right to admit to First Holy Communion?"—*IER,* 5. series, II (1913), 522.

Schlathoelter, F., "First Communion and the Duty of the Confessor"—*AER,* XLVI (1912), 478.

Vermeersch, A., "De Primae Communionis Aetate"—*Periodica,* V (1913), 176.

Zulueta, Francis M., "The Control of Childrens' First Communions"—*AER,* XLVIII (1913), 24.

Periodicals

American Ecclesiastical Review, The, Philadelphia, 1889-1943; Washington, 1944.

Archiv für katholisches Kierchenrecht, Vols. I-VI, Innsbruck, 1857-1861: Vols. VII ——, Mainz, 1862 ——.

Irish Ecclesiastical Record, The, Dublin, 1864 ——.

Jurist, The, Washington, D. C.: The Catholic University of America, 1941 ——.

Ius Pontificium, Romae, 1921 ——.

L'Ami du Clergé, Paris, 1879 ——.

Le Canoniste Contemporain, Paris: P. Litheilleux, 1878-1922.

Periodica de Re Canonica et Morali utili praesertim Religiosis et Missionariis, Brugis, 1905 ——.

ABBREVIATIONS

AAS—*Acta Apostolicae Sedis.*
AER—*American Ecclesiastical Review.*
AKKR—*Archiv für katholisches Kirchenrecht.*
Collectanea—*S. Congregationis de Propaganda Fide.*
Coll. Lac.—*Collectio Lacensis.*
Denzinger—*Enchiridion Symbolorum, etc.*
Fontes—*Codicis Iuris Canonicis . . . Gasparri editi.*
Hardouin—*Acta Conciliorum,* etc.
IER—*Irish Ecclesiastical Record.*
Mansi—*Sacrorum Conciliorum Nova et Amplissima Collectio.*
MPL—Migne, *Patrologia Latina.*
Periodica—*de Re Canonica,* etc.
Thesaurus—*Sacrae Congregationis Concilii Resolutiones.*

ALPHABETICAL INDEX

BIOGRAPHICAL NOTE

MATTHEW M. CROTTY was born September 26, 1919, at The Rower, County Kilkenny, Ireland. He attended The Rower National School, The Christian Brothers' School, New Ross, and St. Kieran's College, Kilkenny. In September, 1938, he was admitted to St. Kieran's Seminary, Kilkenny, where he completed his course in Philosophy and Theology. He was ordained to the Sacred Priesthood on January 30, 1944. In the fall of that year he enrolled in the School of Canon Law of the Catholic University of America, where he received the degree of Baccalaureate in Canon Law in May of 1945, and the degree of Licentiate in Canon Law in June, 1946.

CANON LAW STUDIES *

1. Freriks, Rev. Celestine A., C.PP.S., J.C.D., Religious Congregations in Their External Relations, 121 pp., 1916.
2. Galliher, Rev. Daniel M., O.P., J.C.D., Canonical Elections, 117 pp., 1917.
3. Borkowski, Rev. Aurelius L., O.F.M., J.C.D., De Confraternitatibus Ecclesiasticis, 136 pp., 1918.
4. Castillo, Rev. Cayo, J.C.D., Disertacion Historico-Canonica sobre la Potestad del Cabildo en Sede Vacante o Impedida del Vicario Capitular, 99 pp., 1919 (1918).
5. Kubelbeck, Rev. William J., S.T.B., J.C.D., The Sacred Penitentiaria and Its Relation to Faculties of Ordinaries and Priests, 129 pp., 1918.
6. Petrovits, Rev. Joseph, J.C., S.T.D., J.C.D., The New Church Law on Matrimony, X-461 pp., 1919.
7. Hickey, Rev. John J., S.T.B., J.C.D., Irregularities and Simple Impediments in the New Code of Canon Law, 100 pp., 1920.
8. Klekotka, Rev. Peter J., S.T.B., J.C.D., Diocesan Consultors, 179 pp., 1920.
9. Wanenmacher, Rev. Francis, J.C.D., The Evidence in Ecclesiastical Procedure Affecting the Marriage Bond, 1920 (Printed 1935).
10. Golden, Rev. Henry Francis, J.C.D., Parochial Benefices in the New Code, IV-119 pp., 1921 (Printed 1925).
11. Koudelka, Rev. Charles J., J.C.D., Pastors, Their Rights and Duties According to the New Code of Canon Law, 211 pp., 1921.
12. Melo, Rev. Antonius, O.F.M., J.C.D., De Exemptione Regularium, X-188 pp., 1921.
13. Schaaf, Rev. Valentine Theodore, O.F.M., S.T.B., J.C.D., The Cloister. X-180 pp., 1921.
14. Burke, Rev. Thomas Joseph, S.T.D., J.C.D., Competence in Ecclesiastical Tribunals, IV-117 pp., 1922.
15. Leech, Rev. George Leo, J.C.D., A Comparative Study of the Constitution "Apostolicae Sedis" and the "Codex Juris Canonici," 179 pp., 1922.
16. Motry, Rev. Hubert Louis, S.T.D., J.C.D., Diocesan Faculties According to the Code of Canon Law, II-167 pp., 1922.
17. Murphy, Rev. George Lawrence, J.C.D., Delinquencies and Penalties in the Administration and the Reception of the Sacraments, IV-121 pp., 1923.
18. O'Reilly, Rev. John Anthony, S.T.B., J.C.D., Ecclesiastical Sepulture in the New Code of Canon Law, II-129 pp., 1923.

* From nn. 1-100 inclusive only n. 25 is still obtainable.
From n. 101 onward all numbers are available except the following: nn. 101-114 inclusive, and also nn. 116, 118, 120, 122, 123 and 162.

19. Michalicka, Rev. Wenceslas Cyrill, O.S.B., J.C.D., Judicial Procedure in Dismissal of Clerical Exempt Religious, 107 pp., 1923.
20. Dargin, Rev. Edward Vincent, S.T.B., J.C.D., Reserved Cases According to the Code of Canon Law, IV-103 pp., 1924.
21. Godfrey, Rev. John A., S.T.B., J.C.D., The Right of Patronage According to the Code of Canon Law, 153 pp., 1924.
22. Hagedorn, Rev. Francis Edward, J.C.D., General Legislation on Indulgences, II-154 pp., 1924.
23. King, Rev. James Ignatius, J.C.D., The Administration of the Sacraments to Dying Non-Catholics, V-141 pp., 1924.
24. Winslow, Rev. Francis Joseph, O.F.M., J.C.D., Vicars and Prefects Apostolic, IV-149 pp., 1924.
25. Correa, Rev. Jose Servelion, S.T.L., J.C.D., La Potestad Legislativa de la Iglesia Catolica, IV-127 pp., 1925.
26. Dugan, Rev. Henry Francis, A.M., J.C.D., The Judiciary Department of the Diocesan Curia, 87 pp., 1925.
27. Keller, Rev. Charles Frederick, S.T.B., J.C.D., Mass Stipends, 167 pp., 1925.
28. Paschang, Rev. John Linus, J.C.D., The Sacramentals According to the Code of Canon Law, 129 pp., 1925.
29. Piontek, Rev. Cyrillus, O.F.M., S.T.B., J.C.D., De Indulto Exclaustrationis necnon Saecularizationis, XIII-289 pp., 1925.
30. Kearney, Rev. Richard Joseph, S.T.B., J.C.D., Sponsors at Baptism According to the Code of Canon Law, IV-127 pp., 1925.
31. Bartlett, Rev. Chester Joseph, A.M., LL.B., J.C.D., The Tenure of Parochial Property in the United States of America, V-108 pp., 1926.
32. Kilker, Rev. Adrian Jerome, J.C.D., Extreme Unction, V-425 pp., 1926.
33. McCormick, Rev. Robert Emmett, J.C.D., Confessors of Religious, VIII-266 pp., 1926.
34. Miller, Rev. Newton Thomas, J.C.D., Founded Masses According to the Code of Canon Law, VII-93 pp., 1926.
35. Roelker, Rev. Edward G., S.T.D., J.C.D., Principles of Privilege According to the Code of Canon Law, XI-166 pp., 1926.
36. Bakalarczyk, Rev. Richardus, M.I.C., J.U.D., De Novitiatu, VIII-208 pp., 1927.
37. Pizzuti, Rev. Lawrence, O.F.M., J.U.L., De Parochis Religiosis, 1927. (Not Printed.)
38. Bliley, Rev. Nicholas Martin, O.S.B., J.C.D., Altars According to the Code of Canon Law, XIX-132 pp., 1927.
39. Brown, Mr. Brendan Francis, A.B., LL.M., J.U.D., The Canonical Juristic Personality with Special Reference to its Status in the United States of America, V-212 pp., 1927.
40. Cavanaugh, Rev. William Thomas, C.P., J.U.D., The Reservation of the Blessed Sacrament, VIII-101 pp., 1927.

41. DOHENY, REV. WILLIAM J., C.S.C., A.B., J.U.D., Church Property: Modes of Acquisition, X-118 pp., 1927.
42. FELDHAUS, REV. ALOYSIUS H., C.PP.S., J.C.D., Oratories, IX-141 pp., 1927.
43. KELLY, REV. JAMES PATRICK, A.B., J.C.D., The Jurisdiction of the Simple Confessor, X-208 pp., 1927.
44. NEUBERGER, REV. NICHOLAS J., J.C.D., Canon 6 or the Relation of the Codex Juris Canonici to the Preceding Legislation, V-95 pp., 1927.
45. O'KEEFE, REV. GERALD MICHAEL, J.C.D., Matrimonial Dispensations, Powers of Bishops, Priests, and Confessors, VIII-232 pp., 1927.
46. QUIGLEY, REV. JOSEPH A. M., A.B., J.C.D., Condemned Societies, 139 pp., 1927.
47. ZAPLOTNIK, REV. JOHANNES LEO, J.C.D., De Vicariis Foraneis, X-142 pp., 1927.
48. DUSKIE, REV. JOHN ALOYSIUS, A.B., J.C.D., The Canonical Status of the Orientals in the United States, VIII-196 pp., 1928.
49. HYLAND, REV. FRANCIS EDWARD, J.C.D., Excommunication, Its Nature, Historical Development and Effects, VIII-181 pp., 1928.
50. REINMANN, REV. GERALD JOSEPH, O.M.C., J.C.D., The Third Order Secular of Saint Francis, 201 pp., 1928.
51. SCHENK, REV. FRANCIS J., J.C.D., The Matrimonial Impediments of Mixed Religion and Disparity of Cult, XVI-318 pp., 1929.
52. COADY, REV. JOHN JOSEPH, S.T.D., J.U.D., A.M., The Appointment of Pastors, VIII-150 pp., 1929.
53. KAY, REV. THOMAS HENRY, J.C.D., Competence in Matrimonial Procedure, VIII-164 pp., 1929.
54. TURNER, REV. SIDNEY JOSEPH, C.P., J.U.D., The Vow of Poverty, XLIX-217 pp., 1929.
55. KEARNEY, REV. RAYMOND A., A.B., S.T.D., J.C.D., The Principles of Delegation, VII-149 pp., 1929.
56. CONRAN, REV. EDWARD JAMES, A.B., J.C.D., The Interdict, V-163 pp., 1930.
57. O'NEILL, REV. WILLIAM H., J.C.D., Papal Rescripts of Favor, VII-218 pp., 1930.
58. BASTNAGEL, REV. CLEMENT VINCENT, J.U.D., The Appointment of Parochial Adjutants and Assistants, XV-257 pp., 1930.
59. FERRY, REV. WILLIAM A., A.B., J.C.D., Stole Fees, V-136 pp., 1930.
60. COSTELLO, REV. JOHN MICHAEL, A.B., J.C.D., Domicile and Quasi-Domicile, VII-201 pp., 1930.
61. KREMER, REV. MICHAEL NICHOLAS, A.B., S.T.B., J.C.D., Church Support in the United States, VI-136 pp., 1930.
62. ANGULO, REV. LUIS, C.M., J.C.D., Legislation de la Iglesia sobre la intencion en la application de la Santa Misa, VII-104 pp., 1931.
63. FREY, REV. WOLFGANG NORBERT, O.S.B., A.B., J.C.D., The Act of Religious Profession, VIII-174 pp., 1931.

64. Roberts, Rev. James Brendan, A.B., J.C.D., The Banns of Marriage, XIV-140 pp., 1931.
65. Ryder, Rev. Raymond Aloysius, A.B., J.C.D., Simony, IX-151 pp., 1931.
66. Campagna, Rev. Angelo, Ph.D., J.U.D., Il Vicario Generale del Vescovo, VII-205 pp., 1931.
67. Cox, Rev. Joseph Godfrey, A.B., J.C.D., The Administration of Seminaries, VI-124 pp., 1931.
68. Gregory, Rev. Donald J., J.U.D., The Pauline Privilege, XV-165 pp., 1931.
69. Donohue, Rev. John F., J.C.D., The Impediment of Crime, VII-110 pp., 1931.
70. Dooley, Rev. Eugene A., O.M.I., J.C.D., Church Law on Sacred Relics, IX-143 pp., 1931.
71. Orth, Rev. Clement Raymond, O.M.C., J.C.D., The Approbation of Religious Institutes, 171 pp., 1931.
72. Pernicone, Rev. Joseph M., A.B., J.C.D., The Ecclesiastical Prohibition of Books, XII-267 pp., 1932.
73. Clinton, Rev. Connell, A.B., J.C.D., The Paschal Precept, IX-108 pp., 1932.
74. Donnelly, Rev. Francis B., A.M., S.T.L., J.C.D., The Diocesan Synod, VIII-125 pp., 1932.
75. Torrente, Rev. Camilo, C.M.F., J.C.D., Las Procesiones Sagradas, V-145 pp., 1932.
76. Murphy, Rev. Edwin J., C.PP.S., J.C.D., Suspension Ex Informata Conscientia, XI-122 pp., 1932.
77. MacKenzie, Rev. Eric F., A.M., S.T.L., J.C.D., The Delict of Heresy in its Commission, Penalization, Absolution, VII-124 pp., 1932.
78. Lyons, Rev. Avitus E., S.T.B., J.C.D., The Collegiate Tribunal of First Instance, XI-147 pp., 1932.
79. Connolly, Rev. Thomas A., J.C.D., Appeals, XI-195, pp., 1932.
80. Sangmeister, Rev. Joseph V., A.B., J.C.D., Force and Fear as Precluding Matrimonial Consent, V-211 pp., 1932.
81. Jaeger, Rev. Leo A., A.B., J.C.D., The Administration of Vacant and Quasi-Vacant Episcopal Sees in the United States, IX-229 pp., 1932.
82. Rimlinger, Rev. Herbert T., J.C.D., Error Invalidating Matrimonial Consent, VII-79 pp., 1932.
83. Barrett, Rev. John D. M., S.S., J.C.D., A Comparative Study of the Councils of Baltimore and the Code of Canon Law, X-223 pp., 1932.
84. Carberry, Rev. John J., Ph.D., S.T.D., J.C.D., The Juridical Form of Marriage, X-177 pp., 1934.
85. Dolan, Rev. John L., A.B., J.C.D., The Defensor Vinculi, XII-157 pp., 1934.
86. Hannan, Rev. Jerome D., A.M., S.T.D., LL.B., J.C.D., The Canon Law of Wills, IX-517 pp., 1934.

87. LEMIEUX, REV. DELISE A., A.M., J.C.D., The Sentence in Ecclesiastical Procedure, IX-131 pp., 1934.
88. O'ROURKE, REV. JAMES J., A.B., J.C.D., Parish Registers, VII-109 pp., 1934.
89. TIMLIN, REV. BARTHOLOMEW, O.F.M., A.M., J.C.D., Conditional Matrimonial Consent, X-381 pp., 1934.
90. WAHL, REV. FRANCIS X., A.B., J.C.D., The Matrimonial Impediments of Consanguinity and Affinity, VI-125 pp., 1934.
91. WHITE, REV. ROBERT J., A.B., LL.B., S.T.B., J.C.D., Canonical Ante-Nuptial Promises and the Civil Law, VI-152 pp., 1934.
92. HERRERA, REV. ANTONIO PARRA, O.C.D., J.C.D., Legislación Ecclesiastica sobra el Ayuno y la Abstinencia, XI-191 pp., 1935.
93. KENNEDY, REV. EDWIN J., J.C.D., The Special Matrimonial Process in Cases of Evident Nullity, X-165 pp., 1935.
94. MANNING, REV. JOHN J., A.B., J.C.D., Presumption of Law in Matrimonial Procedure, XI-111 pp., 1935.
95. MOEDER, REV. JOHN M., J.C.D., The Proper Bishop for Ordination and Dismissorial Letters, VII-135 pp., 1935.
96. O'MARA, REV. WILLIAM A., A.B., J.C.D., Canonical Causes for Matrimonial Dispensations, IX-155 pp., 1935.
97. REILLY, REV. PETER, J.C.D., Residence of Pastors, IX-81 pp., 1935.
98. SMITH, REV. MARINER T., O.P., S.T.Lr., J.C.D., The Penal Law for Religious, VIII-169 pp., 1935.
99. WHALEN, REV. DONALD W., A.M., J.C.D., The Value of Testimonial Evidence in Matrimonial Procedure, XIII-297 pp., 1935.
100. CLEARY, REV. JOSEPH F., J.C.D., Canonical Limitations on the Alienation of Church Property, VIII-141 pp., 1936.
101. GLYNN, REV. JOHN C., J.C.D., The Promoter of Justice, XX-337 pp., 1936.
102. BRENNAN, REV. JAMES H., S.S., M.A., S.T.B., J.C.D., The Simple Convalidation of Marriage, VI-135 pp., 1937.
103. BRUNINI, REV. JOSEPH BERNARD, J.C.D., The Clerical Obligations of Canons 139 and 142, X-121 pp., 1937.
104. CONNOR, REV. MAURICE, A.B., J.C.D., The Administrative Removal of Pastors, VIII-159 pp., 1937.
105. GUILFOYLE, REV. MERLIN JOSEPH, J.C.D., Custom, XI-144 pp., 1937.
106. HUGHES, REV. JAMES AUSTIN, A.B., A.M., J.C.D., Witnesses in Criminal Trials of Clerics, IX-140 pp., 1937.
107. JANSEN, REV. RAYMOND J., A.B., S.T.L., J.C.D., Canonical Provisions for Catechetical Instruction, VII-153 pp., 1937.
108. KEALY, REV. JOHN JAMES, A.B., J.C.D., The Introductory Libellus in Church Court Procedure, XI-121 pp., 1937.
109. MCMANUS, REV. JAMES EDWARD, C.SS.R., J.C.D., The Administration of Temporal Goods in Religious Institutes, XVI-196 pp., 1937.

110. Moriarty, Rev. Eugene James, J.C.D., Oaths in Ecclesiastical Courts, X-115 pp., 1937.
111. Rainer, Rev. Eligius George, C.SS.R., J.C.D., Suspension of Clerics, XVII-249 pp., 1937.
112. Reilly, Rev. Thomas F., C.SS.R., J.C.D., Visitation of Religious, VI-195 pp., 1938.
113. Moriarty, Rev. Francis E., C.SS.R., J.C.D., The Extraordinary Absolution from Censures, XV-334 pp., 1938.
114. Connolly, Rev. Nicholas P., J.C.D., The Canonical Erection of Parishes, X-132 pp., 1938.
115. Donovan, Rev. James Joseph, J.C.D., The Pastor's Obligation in Prenuptial Investigation, XII-322 pp., 1938.
116. Harrigan, Rev. Robert J., M.A., S.T.B., J.C.D., The Radical Sanation of Invalid Marriages, VIII-208 pp., 1938.
117. Boffa, Rev. Conrad Humbert, J.C.D., Canonical Provisions for Catholic Schools, VII-211 pp., 1939.
118. Parsons, Rev. Anscar John, O.M.Cap., J.C.D., Canonical Elections, XII-236 pp., 1939.
119. Reilly, Rev. Edward Michael, A.B., J.C.D., The General Norms of Dispensation, XII-156 pp., 1939.
120. Ryan, Rev. Gerald Aloysius, A.B., J.C.D., Principles of Episcopal Jurisdiction, XII-172 pp., 1939.
121. Burton, Rev. Francis James, C.S.C., A.B., J.C.D., A Commentary on Canon 1125, X-222 pp., 1940.
122. Miaskiewicz, Rev. Francis Sigismund, J.C.D., Supplied Jurisdiction According to Canon 209, XII-340 pp., 1940.
123. Rice, Rev. Patrick William, A.B., J.C.D., Proof of Death in Prenuptial Investigation, VIII-156 pp., 1940.
124. Anglin, Rev. Thomas Francis, M.S., J.C.D., The Eucharistic Fast, VIII-183 pp., 1941.
125. Coleman, Rev. John Jerome, J.C.D., The Minister of Confirmation, VI-153 pp., 1941.
126. Downs, Rev. John Emmanuel, A.B., J.C.D., The Concept of Clerical Immunity, XI-163 pp., 1941.
127. Esswein, Rev. Anthony Albert, J.C.D., Extrajudicial Penal Powers of Ecclesiastical Superiors, X-144 pp., 1941.
128. Farrell, Rev. Benjamin Francis, M.A., S.T.L., J.C.D., The Rights and Duties of the Local Ordinary Regarding Congregations of Women Religious of Pontifical Approval, V-195 pp., 1941.
129. Feeney, Rev. Thomas John, A.B., S.T.L., J.C.D., Restitutio in Integrum, VI-169 pp., 1941.
130. Findlay, Rev. Stephen William, O.S.B., A.B., J.C.D., Canonical Norms Governing the Deposition and Degradation of Clerics, XVII-279 pp., 1941.

131. Goodwine, Rev. John, A.B., S.T.L., J.C.D., The Right of the Church to Acquire Property, VIII-119 pp., 1941.
132. Heston, Rev. Edward Louis, C.S.C., Ph.D., S.T.D., J.C.D., The Alienation of Church Property in the United States, XII-222 pp., 1941.
133. Hogan, Rev. James John, A.B., S.T.L., J.C.D., Judicial Advocates and Procurators, XIII-200 pp., 1941.
134. Kealy, Rev. Thomas M., A.B., Litt.B., J.C.D., Dowry of Women Religious, IX-152 pp., 1941.
135. Keene, Rev. Michael James, O.S.B., J.C.D., Religious Ordinaries and Canon 198, V-164 pp., 1942.
136. Kerin, Rev. Charles A., S.S., M.A., S.T.B., J.C.D., The Privation of Christian Burial, XVI-279 pp., 1941.
137. Louis, Rev. William Francis, M.A., J.C.D., Diocesan Archives, X-101 pp., 1941.
138. McDevitt, Rev. Gilbert Joseph, A.B., J.C.D., Legitimacy and Legitimation, X-247 pp., 1941.
139. McDonough, Rev. Thomas Joseph, A.B., J.C.D., Apostolic Administrators, X-217 pp., 1941.
140. Meier, Rev. Carl Anthony, A.B., J.C.D., Penal Administrative Procedüre Against Negligent Pastors, XI-240 pp., 1941.
141. Schmidt, Rev. John Rogg, A.B., J.C.D., The Principles of Authentic Interpretation in Canon 17 of the Code of Canon Law, XII-331 pp., 1941.
142. Slafkosky, Rev. Andrew Leonard, A.B., J.C.D., The Canonical Episcopal Visitation of the Diocese, X-197 pp., 1941.
143. Swoboda, Rev. Innocent Robert, O.F.M., J.C.D., Ignorance in Relation to the Imputability of Delicts, IX-271 pp., 1941.
144. Dubé, Rev. Arthur Joseph, A.B., J.C.D., The General Principles for the Reckoning of Time in Canon Law, VIII-299 pp., 1941.
145. McBride, Rev. James T., A.B., J.C.D., Incardination and Excardination of Seculars, XX-585 pp., 1941.
146. Król, Rev. John T., J.C.D., The Defendant in Ecclesiastical Trials, XII-207 pp., 1942.
147. Comyns, Rev. Joseph J., C.SS.R., A.B., J.C.D., Papal and Episcopal Administration of Church Property, XIV-155 pp., 1942.
148. Barry, Rev. Garrett Francis, O.M.I., J.C.D., Violation of the Cloister, XII-260 pp., 1942.
149. Bolduc, Rev. Gatien, C.S.V., A.B., S.T.L., J.C.D., Les Études dans les Religions Cléricales, VIII-155 pp., 1942.
150. Boyle, Rev. David John, M.A., J.C.D., The Juridic Effects of Moral Certitude on Pre-Nuptial Guarantees, XII-188 pp., 1942.
151. Canavan, Rev. Walter Joseph, M.A., Litt.D., J.C.D., The Profession of Faith, XII-143 pp., 1942.
152. Desrochers, Rev. Bruno, A.B., Ph.L., S.T.B., J.C.D., Le Premier Concile Plénier de Québec et le Code de Droit Canonique, XIV-186 pp., 1942.

153. Dillon, Rev. Robert Edward, A.B., J.C.D., Common Law Marriage, X-148 pp., 1942.
154. Dodwell, Rev. Edward John, Ph.D., S.T.B., J.C.D., The Time and Place for the Celebration of Marriage, X-156 pp., 1942.
155. Donnellan, Rev. Thomas Andrew, A.B., J.C.D., The Obligation of the Missa pro Populo, VII-131 pp., 1942.
156. Eltz, Rev. Louis Anthony, A.B., J.C.D., Cooperation in Crime, XII-208 pp., 1942.
157. Gass, Rev. Sylvester Francis, M.A., J.C.D., Ecclesiastical Pensions, XI-206 pp., 1942.
158. Guiniven, Rev. John Joseph, C.SS.R., J.C.D., The Precept of Hearing Mass, XIV-188 pp., 1942.
159. Gulczynski, Rev. John Theophilus, J.C.D., The Desecration and Violation of Churches, X-126 pp., 1942.
160. Hammill, Rev. John Leo, M.A., J.C.D., The Obligations of the Traveler According to Canon 14, VIII-204 pp., 1942.
161. Haydt, Rev. John Joseph, A.B., J.C.D., Reserved Benefices, XI-148 pp., 1942.
162. Huser, Rev. Roger John, O.F.M., A.B., J.C.D., The Crime of Abortion in Canon Law, XII-187 pp., 1942.
163. Kearney, Rev. Francis Patrick, A.B., S.T.L., J.C.D., The Principles of Canon 1127, X-162 pp., 1942.
164. Linahen, Rev. Leo James, S.T.L., J.C.D., De Absolutione Complicis in Peccato Turpi, V-114 pp., 1942.
165. McCloskey, Rev. Joseph Aloysius, A.B., J.C.D., The Subject of Ecclesiastical Law According to Canon 12, XVII-246 pp., 1942.
166. O'Neill, Rev. Francis Joseph, C.SS.R., J.C.D., The Dismissal of Religious in Temporary Vows, XIII-220 pp., 1942.
167. Prince, Rev. John Edward, A.B., S.T.B., J.C.D., The Diocesan Chancellor, X-136 pp., 1942.
168. Riesner, Rev. Albert Joseph, C.SS.R., J.C.D., Apostates and Fugitives from Religious Institutes, IX-168 pp., 1942.
169. Stenger, Rev. Joseph Bernard, J.C.D., The Mortgaging of Church Property, 186 pp., 1942.
170. Waldron, Rev. Joseph Francis, A.B., J.C.D., The Minister of Baptism, XII-197 pp., 1942.
171. Willett, Rev. Robert Albert, J.C.D., The Probative Value of Documents in Ecclesiastical Trials, X-124 pp., 1942.
172. Woeber, Rev. Edward Martin, M.A., J.C.D., The Interpellations, XII-161 pp., 1942.
173. Benko, Rev. Matthew Aloysius, O.S.B., M.A., J.C.D., The Abbot *Nullius*, XVI-148 pp., 1943.
174. Christ, Rev. Joseph James, M.A., S.T.L., J.C.D., Dispensation from Vindicative Penalties, XIV-285 pp., 1943.

175. Clancy, Rev. Patrick M. J., O.P., A.B., S.T.Lr., J.C.D., The Local Religious Superior, X-229 pp., 1943.
176. Clarke, Rev. Thomas James, J.C.D., Parish Societies, XII-147 pp., 1943.
177. Connolly, Rev. John Patrick, S.T.L., J.C.D., Synodal Examiners and Parish Priest Consultors, X-223 pp., 1943.
178. Drumm, Rev. William Martin, A.B., J.C.D., Hospital Chaplains, XII-175 pp., 1943.
179. Flanagan, Rev. Bernard Joseph, A.B., S.T.L., J.C.D., The Canonical Erection of Religious Houses, X-147 pp., 1943.
180. Kelleher, Rev. Stephen Joseph, A.B., S.T.B., J.C.D., Discussions with Non-Catholics: Canonical Legislation, X-93 pp., 1943.
181. Lewis, Rev. Gordian, C.P., J.C.D., Chapters in Religious Institutes, XII-169 pp., 1943.
182. Marx, Rev. Adolph, J.C.D., The Declaration of Nullity of Marriages Contracted Outside the Church, X-151 pp., 1943.
183. Matulenas, Rev. Raymond Anthony, O.S.B., A.B., J.C.D., Communication, a Source of Privileges, XII-225 pp., 1943.
184. O'Leary, Rev. Charles Gerard, C.SS.R., J.C.D., Religious Dismissed After Perpetual Profession, X-213 pp., 1943.
185. Power, Rev. Cornelius Michael, J.C.D., The Blessing of Cemeteries, XII-231 pp., 1943.
186. Shuhler, Rev. Ralph Vincent, O.S.A., J.C.D., Privileges of Religious to Absolve and Dispense, XII-195 pp., 1943.
187. Ziolkowski, Rev. Thaddeus Stanislaus, A.B., J.C.D., The Consecration and Blessing of Churches, XII-151 pp., 1943.
188. Heneghan, Rev. John Joseph, S.T.D., J.C.D., The Marriages of Unworthy Catholics: Canons 1065 and 1066, XVI-213 pp., 1944.
189. Carroll, Rev. Coleman Francis, M.A., S.T.L., J.C.L., Charitable Institutions.
190. Ciesluk, Rev. Joseph Edward, Ph.B., S.T.L., J.C.L., National Parishes in the United States.
191. Coburn, Rev. Vincent Paul, A.B., J.C.D., Marriages of Conscience, XII-172 pp., 1944.
192. Connors, Rev. Charles Paul, C.S.Sp., A.B., J.C.D., Extra-Judicial Procurators in the Code of Canon Law, X-94 pp., 1944.
193. Coyle, Rev. Paul Raymond, A.B., J.C.D., Judicial Exceptions, X-142 pp., 1944.
194. Fair, Rev. Bartholomew Francis, A.B., S.T.L., J.C.D., The Impediment of Abduction, XII-122 pp., 1944.
195. Gallagher, Rev. Thomas Raphael, O.P., A.B., S.T.Lr., J.C.D., The Examination of the Qualities of the Ordinand, X-166 pp., 1944.
196. Gannon, Rev. John Mark, S.T.L., J.C.D., The Interstices Required for the Promotion to Orders, XII-100 pp., 1944.

197. Goldsmith, Rev. J. William, B.C.S., S.T.L., J.C.D., The Competence of Church and State Over Marriages—Disputed Points, X-128 pp., 1944.

198. Goodwine, Rev. Joseph Gerard, A.B., S.T.B., J.C.D., The Reception of Converts, XIV-326 pp., 1944.

199. Kowalski, Rev. Romuald Eugene, O.F.M., A.B., J.C.D., Sustenance of Religious Houses of Regulars, X-174 pp., 1944.

200. McCoy, Rev. Alan Edward, O.F.M., J.C.D., Force and Fear in Relation to Delictual Imputability and Penal Responsibility, XII-160 pp., 1944.

201. McDevitt, Rev. Vincent John, Ph.B., S.T.L., J.C.L., Perjury.

202. Martin, Rev. Thomas Owen, Ph.D., S.T.D., J.C.D., Adverse Possession, Prescription and Limitation of Actions: The Canonical "Praescriptio," XX-208 pp., 1944.

203. Miklosovic, Rev. Paul John, A.B., J.C.L., Attempted Marriages and Their Consequent Juridic Effects.

204. Mundy, Rev. Thomas Maurice, A.B., S.T.L., J.C.D., The Union of Parishes, X-164 pp., 1944.

205. O'Dea, Rev. John Coyle, A.B., J.C.D., The Matrimonial Impediment of Nonage, VIII-126 pp., 1944.

206. Olalia, Rev. Alexander Ayson, S.T.L., J.C.D., A Comparative Study of the Christian Constitution of States and the Constitution of the Philippine Commonwealth, XII-136 pp., 1944.

207. Poisson, Rev. Pierre-Marie, C.S.C., A.B., Ph.L., Th.L., J.C.L., Droits Patrimoniaux des Maisons et des Eglises Religieuses.

208. Stadalnikas, Rev. Casimir Joseph, M.I.C., J.C.D., Reservation of Censures, X-141 pp., 1944.

209. Sullivan, Rev. Eugene Henry, S.T.L., J.C.D., Proof of the Reception of the Sacraments, X-165 pp., 1944.

210. Vaughan, Rev. William Edward, J.C.D., Constitutions for Diocesan Courts, X-210 pp., 1944.

211. Paro, Rev. Gino, S.T.D., J.C.L., The Right of Apostolic Legation.

212. Balzer, Rev. Ralph Francis, C.P., J.C.D., The Computation of Time in a Canonical Novitiate, X-227 pp., 1945.

213. Dougherty, Rev. John Whelan, A.B., S.T.L., J.C.D., De Inquisitione Speciali, XII-195 pp., 1945.

214. Dziob, Rev. Michael Walter, J.C.D., The Sacred Congregation for the Oriental Church, XII-181 pp., 1945.

215. Eidenschink, Rev. John Albert, O.S.B., B.A., J.C.D., The Election of Bishops in the Letters of Pope Gregory the Great, VIII-200 pp., 1945.

216. Gill, Rev. Nicholas, C.P., J.C.D., The Spiritual Prefect in Clerical Religious Houses of Study, X-140 pp., 1945.

217. Hynes, Rev. Harry Gerard, S.T.L., J.C.D., The Privileges of Cardinals, XII-183 pp., 1945.

218. McDevitt, Rev. Gerald Vincent, S.T.L., J.C.D., The Renunciation of an Ecclesiastical Office, XIV-179 pp., 1945.

219. Manning, Rev. Joseph Leroy, J.C.D., The Free Conferral of Offices, VII-116 pp., 1945.
220. Meyer, Rev. Louis G., O.S.B., A.B., S.T.B., J.C.D., Alms-gathering by Religious, XII-163 pp., 1945.
221. O'Donnell, Rev. Cletus Francis, M.A., J.C.D., The Marriage of Minors, XII-268 pp., 1945.
222. Prunskis, Rev. Joseph, J.C.D., Comparative Law, Ecclesiastical and Civil, in Lithuanian Concordat, X-161 pp., 1945.
223. Sweeney, Rev. Francis Patrick, C.SS.R., J.C.D., The Reduction of Clerics to the Lay State, X-199 pp., 1945.
224. Vogelpohl, Rev. Henry John, J.C.D., The Simple Impediments to Holy Orders, XVI-190 pp., 1945.
225. Brockhaus, Rev. Thomas Aquinas, O.S.B., J.C.D., Religious who are known as *Conversi,* X-127 pp., 1945.
226. Griese, Rev. Orville Nicholas, S.T.D., J.C.D., Marriage and the Procreation of Offspring, XVI-224 pp., 1945.
227. Boudreaux, Rev. Warren Louis, J.C.L., The *"ab acatholicis nati"* of Canon 1099, § 2.
228. Bowe, Rev. Thomas Joseph, A.B., J.C.L., Religious Superioresses.
229. Diederichs, Rev. Michael Ferdinand, S.C.J., J.C.D., The Jurisdiction of the Latin Ordinaries over their Oriental Subjects, XIV-153 pp., 1946.
230. Dingman, Rev. Maurice John, A.B., S.T.L., J.C.L., The Plaintiff in Contentious Trials.
231. Frison, Rev. Basil, C.M.F., M.Mus., J.C.D., The Retroactivity of Law, X-221 pp., 1946.
232. Galvin, Rev. William Anthony, M.A., J.C.D., The Administrative Transfer of Pastors, XII-288 pp., 1946.
233. Goracy, Rev. Joseph C., J.C.L., The Diriment Matrimonial Impediment of Major Orders.
234. Hale, Rev. Joseph Francis, M.A., S.T.L., J.C.L., The Pastor of Burial.
235. Henry, Rev. Joseph Arthur, A.B., J.C.D., The Mass and Holy Communion: Interritual Law, XII-138 pp., 1946.
236. Linenberger, Rev. Herbert, C.PP.S., J.C.L., The False Denunciation of an Innocent Confessor.
237. Lowry, Rev. James Martin, A.B., J.C.D., Dispensation from Private Vows, XII-216 pp., 1946.
238. Lynch, Rev. George Edward, A.B., S.T.L., J.C.D., Coadjutors and Auxiliaries of Bishops, X-107 pp., 1947.
239. Lynch, Rev. Timothy, M.S.SS.T., J.C.D., Contracts between Bishops and Religious Congregations, XIII-232 pp., 1946.
240. McClunn, Rev. Justin David, A.B., S.T.L., J.C.D., Administrative Recourse, VII-142 pp., 1946.

241. LOHMULLER, REV. MARTIN NICHOLAS, A.B., J.C.D., The Promulgation of Law, XII-140 pp., 1947.
242. McGRATH, REV. JAMES, A.B., J.C.D., The Privilege of the Canon, XII-156 pp., 1946.
243. MARBACH, REV. JOSEPH FRANCIS, A.B., J.C.D., Marriage Legislation for the Catholics of the Oriental Rites in the United States and Canada, XIV-314 pp., 1946.
244. SHIMKUS, REV. BERNARD ALOYSIUS, A.B., J.C.L., The Determination and Transfer of Rite.
245. SMITH, REV. VINCENT MICHAEL, A.B., S.T.L., J.C.L., Ignorance Affecting Matrimonial Consent.
246. WACHTRLE, REV. PAUL ANTHONY, A.B., J.C.L., The Baptism of the Children of Non-Catholics.
247. CROTTY, REV. MATTHEW M., J.C.L., The Recipient of First Holy Communion.
248. EAGLETON, REV. GEORGE, J.C.L., The Quinquennial Faculties, Formula IV.
249. GIBBONS, REV. MARION L., C.M., LL.B., J.C.L., Domicile of the Wife Unlawfully Separated from Her Husband.
250. KELLY. REV. BERNARD M., S.T.L., J.C.L., The Functions Reserved to Pastors.
251. KILCULLEN, REV. THOMAS J., LL.M., J.C.L., The Collegiate Moral Person as Party Litigant.
252. LAFONTAINE, REV. GERMAIN J., W.F., J.C.L., Relations Canoniques entre Le Missionnaire et Ses Superieurs.
253. LANE, REV. LORAS T., A.B., S.T.L., J.C.L., Matrimonial Procedure in the Ordinary Court of Second Instance.
254. LOVER, REV. JAMES F., C.SS.R., J.C.L., The Master of Novices.
255. McNICHOLAS, REV. TIMOTHY J., J.C.L., The *Septimae Manus* Witness.
256. MAROSITZ, REV. JOSEPH J., M.S.C., J.C.L., Obligations and Privileges of Religious Promoted to the Episcopal or Cardinalitial Dignities.
257. MURPHY, REV. FRANCIS J., A.B., J.C.L., Legislative Powers of the Provincial Council.
258. O'BRIEN, REV. ROMAEUS W., O. Carm., J.C.L., The Provincial Superior in Religious Orders of Men.
259. PFALLER, REV. BENEDICT A., O.S.B., J.C.L., The *Ipso facto* Effected Dismissal of Religious.
260. POPEK, REV. ALPHONSE S., M.A., J.C.L., The Rights and Obligations of Metropolitans.
261. RISTUCCIA, REV. BERNARD J., C.M., J.C.L., Quasi-Religious.
262. SONNTAG, REV. NATHANIEL L., O.F.M. Cap., J.C.L., Censorship of Special Classes of Books.
263. STADLER, REV. JOSEPH N., J.C.L., Frequent Holy Communion.
264. SZAL, REV. IGNATIUS J., J.C.L., The Communication of Catholics with Schismatics.
265. WAGNER, REV. URBAN S., O.F.M. Conv., J.C.L., Parochial Substitute Vicars and Supplying Priests.

www.ingramcontent.com/pod-product-compliance
Lightning Source LLC
LaVergne TN
LVHW050216080826

844660LV00012B/417
9780813224251